IN GOD'S IMAGE

Reflections on Identity, Human Wholeness and the Authority of Scripture

Edited by
Janet Crawford and Michael Kinnamon

World Council of Churches, Geneva

Cover design: Karen Foget

ISBN No. 2-8254-0767-4

Printed in Switzerland

Contents

INTRODUCTION

"For me, the Community Study is a veritable test of our faith and of the ecumenical movement, a movement which is concerned about the unity of the whole People of God."

Philip Potter
General Secretary
World Council of Churches

Few studies of the World Council of Churches (WCC) have involved more people, generated more interest, or provoked more controversy than the Study on the Community of Women and Men in the Church. The purpose of this small volume is to make available, for the first time, some of the Community Study's richest material on themes that concern not only professional theologians but all Christians: personal identity, human wholeness, and the authority of Scripture.

The first purpose of the WCC, of the entire ecumenical movement, is to call the churches to make visible the unity that is ours in Christ. But what kind of unity are we seeking? What renewal is needed in the church before genuine, lasting unity among Christians can be achieved? The Nairobi Assembly of the WCC (1975) took important steps towards answering these questions, not least when it addressed the issue of women and their role in the body of Christ.

> The Church's unity (said Nairobi) includes women and men in a true mutuality. As a result of rapid cultural, economic and social change, women (and many men) reject the passive or restrictive roles formerly assigned to women, and search for fuller participation in the life of the Church and in society at large. The relations of women and men must be shaped by reciprocity and not by subordination. The unity of the Church requires that women be free

> to live out the gifts which God has given to them and to respond to their calling to share fully in the life and witness of the Church.

In order to support and develop this conviction, the Assembly invited the churches to participate in a new kind of study process, one which took "experience", especially the newly articulated experiences of women, as its major point of departure. In many ways, the methodology of the Community Study was as significant as the results it produced; certainly the two cannot be separated. This methodology, writes Mary Tanner, moderator of the Community Study's advisory committee:

> ... was based on the conviction that our experience of life–whoever we are, wherever we live, whatever church we belong to –is vital raw material for understanding Christian truth and for our vision of the community we seek. But such experience has always to be measured against the Christian tradition which has come down to us through the centuries and which is given to us in and through the teaching, life and witness of the Christian communities to which we belong. That inherited tradition must judge and speak to our experience. But, in its turn, reflection upon our experience as women and men in community helps us to perceive ever fresh the creative insights in that tradition... This theological method of continual interplay between experience and tradition and between tradition and experience lay at the basis of the Community Study.

Most WCC studies start from the "top", bringing together experts in a certain field to seek a consensus which can then be discussed in the churches. The Community Study, however, with its emphasis on personal experience, reversed this procedure. The first step in the study programme–which was directed by Dr. Constance Parvey, a Lutheran pastor and theologian from the United States–was the writing of a study book designed to stimulate discussion in local Christian communities. Only 3,000 copies of the study book were produced in Geneva; but within two years, thanks to local initiative, an estimated 65,000 booklets were in print in more than a dozen languages. Local groups were invited by the study book to send reports of their work to Geneva. More than 150 reports were received, coming from all parts of the world. Regional meetings were also held in Asia (1978), the Middle East (1980), Europe (1980), Africa (1980), Latin America (1981) and North America (1981), each producing a substantial body of documentation. Excerpts from the reports of the local groups and regional meetings that deal with the theme of personal, sexual "identity", make up Part I of this volume.

In addition to local and regional participation, the Community Study also organized three "specialized consultations" to discuss specific theological issues: the ordination of women (August 1979), the concept of human wholeness as derived from reflection on our creation "in the image of God" (September 1980), and scriptural authority (December 1980). The report of the first specialized consultation has been published by the WCC as *The Ordination of Women in Ecumenical Perspective*. The reports on human wholeness and scriptural authority form Parts II and III of this book. We are grateful for the invaluable help we received from Dr. Parvey in the preparation of all these reports for publication.

Finally, input from the various levels of the Community Study–local groups, regional meetings, specialized consultations–provided the background for an international consultation held in Sheffield, England, in July 1981. For ten days the 140 invited participants (two-thirds of them women), along with consultants, observers and staff, explored the following seven issues that were frequently raised in the local and regional responses to the study:

Identity and Relationships in New Community
Marriage, Family and Life Style in New Community
Scripture in New Community
Ministry and Worship in New Community
Authority and Church Structures in New Community
Tradition and Traditions–A Chance for Renewal?
Justice and Freedom in New Community

They also worshipped together, learned from other cultures (the participants came from 90 member churches and more than 50 countries), shared their struggles and hopes, and, for a short time, experienced some measure of what it means to live as a new community of women and men in the church. *The Sheffield Report,* edited by Constance Parvey, has been published by the WCC and Fortress Press (USA). It may be one of the most significant documents to come from the World Council in the period between the Nairobi (1975) and Vancouver (1983) Assemblies.

The Community Study was, of course, a sign and product of its age. If the 1960s were a time when the churches began to realize their role in perpetuating racism, then the 1970s were a time for broadening that focus with a new understanding of the churches' implication in sexism–the systematic and continuous subordination of women on the basis of their sex. The Community Study certainly drew inspiration and nourishment from the feminist movement which achieved momentum during this decade, especially in western societies. But it must be emphasized that the fundamental purpose of the study was not to provide a feminist critique of Christianity, but to explore issues and models of community–authentic, participatory community–through dialogue between men and women in the church. It was necessary for the study to begin, in the words of Philip Potter, with "an exposé of our broken relationships caused by institutionalized male domination"; but it deliberately moved beyond this to ask the positive question: How can women and men present a vision of human wholeness–a vision rooted in both Christian tradition and contemporary experience–which will help in the ecumenical task of renewing the church? The Community Study was–and is–at the very heart of the ecumenical agenda. It reflects the realization that the world will come to believe not because of the clarity of our doctrinal formulations (important as this is), but because of the quality of our life as a loving, reconciling, inclusive community in Christ.

The three themes treated in this short volume are ones that surfaced time and again at all levels of the Community Study process. "Identity" (Part I) may seem like an incredibly broad, amorphous category; but the real issue at stake becomes clear as one reads the voices and hears women speaking for themselves about how different cultures and ideologies have given priority to the life, work and education of men over women.

The impetus for re-evaluating sexual roles and expectations–roles and expectations which hinder many people from reaching their full potential as loving, creative children of God–has come primarily from women; but a number of male participants also realized that they have much to gain from the search for new patterns of identity.

There are many ways in which Part II of this book, the report "Towards a Theology of Human Wholeness", overlaps with the discussion of identity in Part I. It also adds, however, a theological dimension by starting with the question: What does it mean to be created male and female in the image of God (Genesis 1:27f)? The report goes on to explore whether this anthropological starting point can help us to discover or envision the renewed and unified community we seek.

This leads us inevitably to Part III. It can certainly be argued that the issue of "Scriptural Authority in Light of the New Experiences of Women" was central to the entire Community Study. It is here that the methodology of the study process–an interplay between experience and traditional authority–is seen most clearly.

Scripture is normative authority for the church, but many Christians now find that their experience calls them to reject such passages as I Corinthians 11:3-9 (woman created from and for man who is her "head") in favour of genuine mutuality. The issue, of course, is far from clear-cut. Some participants saw Scripture as a word that oppresses, others as the only word that can free and affirm. Most argued that both are true. The discussions on this topic always led to the question of who interprets, and usually to the recommendation that the community of interpreters be expanded to include those (e.g. women) who previously have had little or no authoritative voice in the interpretation of God's Word.

These three issues do not, of course, exhaust the wealth of material gained, or questions raised, during such on extensive study process. For example, the regional meetings in Africa, Asia and Latin America, and the Sheffield consultation, all stressed the need to interrelate the struggles against sexism, racism and class oppression. Not enough research has yet been done on this "web of oppression" to include it as a section in this volume, but it will obviously be an important theme for the WCC in the coming years.

Throughout this introduction we have referred to the Community Study in the past tense. Technically speaking this is accurate since the Community of Women and Men in the Church, as a distinct programme of the WCC, reached the end of its mandate on 31 December 1981. In another sense, however, the study remains very much alive. Its general influence and specific recommendations continue to be felt by all units of the World Council; its issues continue to play an important role in preparations for the Sixth Assembly in Vancouver, and its study book continues to be used by groups in different parts of the world. But, then, this shouldn't be surprising. The search for Christian community "shaped by reciprocity and not by subordination" has really just begun.

The Editors
April, 1983

"Who am I?
Who am I really?
Am I what others want me to be?
Or am I what I would like others to see?
Am I what I think I am
As I wish myself to be, as I should be,
Or am I fearful when I think
that I could be so?
Just a few sure data:
I am a woman, I am 51 years old,
I live alone."

From a local group report

IDENTITY

INTRODUCTION

The most important document for the Study on the Community of Women and Men in the Church was the study book, written in 1978. This 40-page booklet, intended for use by local discussion groups, presented a series of questions on (1) personal and cultural attitudes regarding our identity as women and men, (2) church teachings about women and men in community, and (3) the importance of church structures in the search for new community – questions designed to stimulate exploration "of the vision of the community of women and men in the church which lies at the heart of the Gospel". The study book was widely distributed to member churches of the World Council, to ecumenical and national church councils, to women's organizations and to interested individuals. Originally published in Geneva in English, French and German, it was translated by local initiatives into at least thirteen other languages.

Groups in every region of the world used the study book, which was often adapted to fit local situations and needs. One hundred and fifty of these groups sent reports to the Geneva office. Although exact numbers are not known, it is estimated that over 2,000 people were represented by these responses; and it should be kept in mind that many other groups used the study but, for various reasons, did not send reports to Geneva. The greatest response came from groups in the North Atlantic or "developed" world, but reports were also sent from Asia, Africa, the Middle East, Latin America, the Caribbean and the Pacific.

Note: The editing of this material was done in response to a mandate of the Sub-unit on Women in Church and Society.

Groups were organized on many different bases: there were denominational groups, ecumenical groups, parish or congregational groups, groups of church leaders, of church employees, of "ordinary" church members, groups of theological students, of clergy, of deaconnesses, of married couples, and many groups which combined women and men, young and old, lay and ordained, married and single.

Most member churches of the WCC were represented at some point in the local groups, with the greatest participation coming from members of the main Protestant denominations. Individuals from a number of Orthodox churches took part in ecumenical groups, and a distinctive Orthodox contribution came from several Orthodox congregations as well as from a separate but parallel study programme organized by the Orthodox Church of America. There was also significant Roman Catholic participation in many local discussions.

Participants in those groups sending reports ranged in age from 11 to 85, but the majority were between 35 and 50. Most were married, and a number participated with their spouses. Many described themselves as "middle-class" and, although a wide variety of occupations was represented, the great majority were professionals, "white-collar" workers, or married women without paid employment. Many were engaged in either professional or voluntary church leadership positions. Although the study was designed to promote the renewal of the entire church community–women *and* men–women participants out-numbered men by about two to one.

In short, the "typical" group membership was predominantly female, middle-aged and middle-class. The groups as a whole did not represent poor, uneducated rural or working-class people, nor did they involve many from racial and ethnic minorities. Men and young people did participate, but in relatively small numbers.

The reports from the local study groups range from lengthy documents–well-printed, bound and illustrated–to brief, handwritten summaries. In addition to reports, the reponses included statistical data, bibliographies, personal statements and individual testimonies, sermons, prayers, poetry–even jokes! Some groups met regularly for weeks or months; others met once or twice. Some discussed all of the study book questions and even added new ones; others concentrated on one or two issues. Some emphasized personal experience; others took a more objective, descriptive approach.

A number of groups which worked on the study over a prolonged period reported many strains and frustrations. They commented on the difficulty of really hearing others, the pain of not being heard, the struggle to be open, the threat of change–and also on the foretaste they had of what it might mean to live in a new community of women and men, to be truly "one" in Jesus Christ. In the words of one group from Australia,

> In our lives and in our study the members of this group are deeply and constantly aware of the changing situation of women in relation to the "kingdom". The group reflects both the old patterns and the new possibilities, and experiences the struggles and hurts involved in moving from one to the other... It has been a slow, hard and at times uncomfortable experience of uncovering problems. But we have grown closer and more committed to one another, and our hope has usually been just slightly greater than our despair.

Through the medium of the group reports, these experiences are being shared with others. Unsystematic, unscientific and unacademic as they are, the reports offer an unprecedented wealth of material to the ecumenical movement. In the words of Philip Potter, General Secretary of the World Council of Churches , they are "a sort of algebraic sign of a very great depth of well-buried meaning".

Questions from the study guide were also used as a basis for discussion at the regional meetings held in 1980 and 1981. These meetings–which took place in Africa, Asia, Europe, Latin America, the Middle East and North America–brought together people from a wider area than the local groups. Many regional participants had already taken part in the study in their local congregations.

An analysis of the local and regional reports reveals that the most frequently discussed, and extensively documented, theme is that of *identity*. Participants were eager to share their experiences of what it means to be women or men, to discuss the expectations laid upon them by Church and culture, to comment on the changes and conflicts occurring in their sense of identity, and to share their hopes and visions of new identity. They responded readily to such questions as:

- How would you describe yourself?
- What are the patterns that exist for women and men in your culture?

- What characteristics do we value in women? in men?
- Do women have the same opportunities as men in your church and society?
- Can an exclusively male image of God include the full humanity of both women and men?
- How did the attitude of Jesus towards women differ from the common religious and cultural views of his day?

The following account draws on responses to these (and related) questions from local groups and regional meetings, pointing both to the areas of common experience shared by women and men in different countries and churches, and to the areas of significant difference. As far as possible, the participants speak for themselves, in direct quotations (translated into English where necessary). It should be kept in mind that, while the following material concentrates on the question of identity, the actual reports dealt with a much wider range of themes and issues.

PERSONAL IDENTITY

A world of change

Underlying both the study questions and the responses is the evident assumption that women and men today live in a world of change. Scientific discoveries and technological advances, economic, political and social changes, processes of urbanization and industrialization are taking place with amazing rapidity, and no area of the world remains untouched. Within this context of change, women and men are responding to new opportunities, making new decisions about the ways they live, experiencing new and different roles, and coming to fresh understandings of who they are and what it means to live as male or female human beings in community. Identity and roles are no longer as fixed as they once seemed, and traditional views of what it means to be woman or man are increasingly questioned, in both society and the church.

One group described several factors which they experienced as contributing to change in the world and in their lives:

- Industrialization and urbanisation transform human relationships, especially within families. The anonymity of the cities, the nuclear family and the employment of women give rise to new patterns of behaviour.

- The industrialized society, in fulfilling material needs, allows us to aspire to "the quality of life". One can devote oneself more to the development of people than to production.
- Widespread access to knowledge, education for all, the chance to obtain professional qualification and the abundance of information supplied by the media add to our cultural richness. This in turn allows for more objective consideration of social models that have been internalized.
- Finally, let us mention the law, which, while responding to needs (parental authority, new rights of women), at the same time accelerates this evolution.

  Thus, the world in which women and men live today has changed so radically that the norms and values which were once necessary and legitimate need to be adapted to the new conditions of civilization. *(France)*

Many groups commented on the uncertainty and tension which they experienced as they lived through change and transition. For some, the process of change involves major conflict as they experience themselves "caught between the world of heritage and the world of imminence" (Trinidad), or "caught between traditional attitudes and modern expectations" (African Regional Report). But there is also, in many reports, a positive note of hope, an envisioning of new identity and new community.

> The old ways of life are being challenged, but the experiences of the new generation are sometimes laden with anguish. This feeling of insecurity is general, but on the other hand it raises real expectations for more just and more genuine relationships. *(Switzerland)*

Sexual identity: male and female

As human beings we all, male and female, belong to the same human species, and yet few of the study participants thought of themselves primarily as *human*. Rather, in the words of one group,

> Most of us seemed to start at the point of our male-female sexual identity. Few of us thought of ourselves first as people, as human beings who happened to be secondarily male or female. *(New Zealand)*

One report explored the genetic basis for this differentiation of male and female:

> Looking at the history of living organisms we find that early forms of life multiply by binary fission, simply splitting into two identical organisms, and some of the most primitive of these, such as amoebae, still multiply themselves in this way. In evolutionary terms, a more advanced stage comes when the new organism is formed from the union of two separate cells, each with a different complement of genetic material or chromosomes. This is what happens in all mammals. Present-day knowledge indicates that the X and Y chromosomes determine the sex of a human being and that each parent contributes half of the chromosomes needed to make up a complete and original combination for their offspring. The female cells all have X chromosomes. The male sex cells are of two kinds, one containing the X or female determining factor, and the other containing the Y or male determining factor. These are present in the male semen in approximately equal numbers. Thus when the egg cell receives an X sperm it will develop into a female, when a Y sperm it will develop into a male. *(Great Britain, published as God's Yes to Sexuality)*

Because of this difference in chromosomes, human beings are born as male or female, having bodies with biological similarities and differences which can be observed, measured and assessed. The report goes on to observe, however, that according to recent research:

> It is a matter of obscurity to what extent the physical differences in sexual organs, hormones, body build and so on mirror basic differences in the psychological, intellectual or spiritual spheres. Some would urge that, just as a bleached human bone found on the shore, or a single blood cell proclaim their sex to the scientific analyst, so in the region of the mind and imagination, the sex of the person deeply conditions every part of that person's knowledge and experience. Others would protest that this goes too far, being consequent upon centuries of cultural pressure to over-polarize the sexes.

Cultural identity: masculine and feminine

The group reports clearly reflect a basic division of opinion between those who believe that identity as male or female is determined largely by the biological difference between the sexes, and those who hold that it is more a matter of cultural conditioning and learned behaviour. There was, however, considerable agreement among the groups that, whether culturally conditioned or innate, certain characteristics and traits are considered to be "masculine" and others "feminine". Furthermore, there was a remarkable degree of cross-cultural agreement on these characteristics, as the following examples illustrate:

Masculine characteristics	*Feminine characteristics*
objective	subjective
logical	illogical
strong	weak
simple	complex
	(German Democratic Republic)
active	passive
dominating	dependent
	(Sweden)
strong	weak
independent	dependent
decisive	indecisive
rational	emotional
intelligent	beautiful
active	passsive
dominant	fragile
realistic	impulsive
	(Latin American Regional Report)

One group summarized advertisements for employment as a way of illustrating differences between "ideal" masculine and feminine characteristics:

> HE is dynamic, eager to pitch in and get started, has the ability to get what he wants, the will to succeed, is able to motivate others and get them working, is fit, performance-oriented and resolute. He has great presence and is ready to take on responsibility. He has leadership ability, can think in abstracts, handle stress, is flexible and has tactical ability. Energy, imagination and creativity are expected of him.
>
> SHE has organizational talent, is reliable, conscientious and loves human contact, is courteous, relaxed and sure of herself in public, clever and well-groomed. She is friendly, charming and chic. She

> is flexible, intelligent and openminded, has a good all-round education, likes work, is loyal and has a well-balanced personality. *(Federal Republic of Germany)*

From these examples it is clear that there is a common tendency to attribute different charactistics to the two sexes, and that such differentiation is often seen in terms of opposition or polarity. In general, masculine characteristics are related to activity, strength, and rationality, while feminine characteristics are related to passivity, weakness, and emotion.

Some groups accepted masculine and feminine characteristics as innate, constitutive elements of male and female identity, attributes corresponding directly to biological, sexual differences. Men have, or should have, masculine characteristics, while women have, or should have, feminine characteristics. Orthodox groups in particular expressed the understanding that there are profound and permanent differences between women and men; this, they contended, is the Creator's will for humankind, the two sexes being complementary.

> The inexpressible, indefinable differences between people arise from the fact that they belong to different sexes. This is the Creator's will according to the Genesis narrative. *(France)*

> For man and woman complement each other and all are one in Christ. *(Lebanon)*

Other groups took a more questioning stance:

> Are there male and female characteristics? Do women have richer intuition, stronger maternal feelings, and men more determination and logical thinking? Although this is frequently presupposed it is not guaranteed that these are innate characteristics. *(Czechoslovakia)*

Most groups, howerer, agreed with the opinion of the Asian Regional Report that "except for biological differences, all other differences are culturally, socially and economically determined". According to another group,

> More objective work now sees these (masculine and feminine) characteristics distributed in great variety among all human beings, and both men and women are found to have characteristics which at one time, or in another culture, would have been associated with the other sex. *(Great Britain)*

Working along the same lines, a group in the United States used an "androgyny scale" supplied by a psychologist to place themselves on a "masculine/feminine" continuum. Most members of the group found that on this scale they had a considerable number of both masculine and feminine traits.

Inferiority and superiority

Among those groups (the large majority) which maintained that differences between women and men are largely the result of cultural conditioning, there was also considerable agreement that it is generally men who define what it means to be male or female and who assign masculine and feminine characteristics and roles to the sexes. According to these groups, men have traditionally been regarded as superior and dominant beings, women as inferior and subordinate; and this pattern persists despite social changes.

> Men define the desirable female characteristics, physical as well as personal, social and religious qualities. And women accept this as a low status group oriented towards men as a high status group.
>
> *(Sweden)*

A French group wrote of "the established fact of culturally engendered male and female inferiority", but distinguished two different approaches for establishing this. In the first, "la piste d'opposition", woman is seen as the negative "other" of man, his rival, enemy, seductress and temptress. In the second, "la piste du fusionnel", woman is also defined by man, but in a more subtle fashion:

> The male takes for himself the right to speak in the name of humankind, woman being unable to avoid melting into this humanistic and general vision which denies differences.

In both cases, woman is understood as something less than man; but the group insists that "we are talking about a culturally engendered superiority/inferiority, not a natural one".

A woman university graduate from Nigeria gave a poignant testimony to the low status of a woman in her society. Her mother told her,

> "In your father's eyes you are only a child, you are only a girl-child. He considers you as always inferior to him no matter what

> you achieve, no matter how old you become. You are his property."
>
> I later found out that my mother shares the same view, so do other persons I tried to work with...

Several groups commented that "woman's place in society depends on her relationship to a man" (Switzerland) and that woman has no value or worth of her own.

> In many places [woman] has no value in herself, for she is known as the wife, the sister or the daughter of a certain man. Even more, she would be of no consequence unless she gives birth to a male.
> *(Middle East Regional Report)*

> We feel that society always sees a woman in relation to or in terms of something or someone else, according to a scale of values preconceived in a male superiority framework. For example, she is looked upon as a wife, in relation to her husband; as a mother, in relation to her children; as a nun in relation to the church.
> *(Latin American Regional Report)*

> We no longer want to be "the shadow of our husbands" but want to be recognized for ourselves. We want to be "somebody" and not "related to somebody". *(Switzerland)*

Others pointed out that women are often considered as objects or possessions, rather than as persons.

> Women serve the interest of the male-dominated society... [They are] primarily tools of men, useful for sex pleasure and child-bearing, otherwise having simply no place of influence or respect in society... no real voice in the thought, power, or direction of that society... *(India)*

> The common opinion today is that the woman is the husband's property and this is reinforced both by men and by the ignorance of women. *(African Regional Report)*

Even at birth, boy babies are frequently valued more highly than girls, thus beginning a life-long pattern of male superiority.

> A father, whose oldest child was a girl, heard at the time of his son's birth: "Now you are really a father". Apparently, it doesn't mean much to be the father of a girl. *(FRG)*

Cultural conditioning

If, as some groups held, stereotyped views of masculine and feminine characteristics and behaviour are the result of socialization and cultural conditioning, how does this take place? A number of groups commented on the formal and informal means by which they thought children learned the cultural norms and expectations for women and men. Some agreed with the Latin American Regional Report that "formal education imparted by society perpetuates the division between women and men".

> Choice of subjects at school, and subsequently of careers, is governed by sex... Girls are encouraged to do Arts subjects–to "entertain their husbands' clients". *(England)*

An Indian group studied materials on prejudices in education, which showed that "school girls are depicted as if they are inferior to school boys" and that "children absorb arbitrarily defined sexual roles such as 'boys are brave' and 'girls are pretty'".

The mass media was seen as particularly influential in perpetuating sexual stereotypes; advertising in the media was often criticised for commercializing masculinity and femininity and for treating women as little more than sex objects. A group of high school students in West Germany, for example, spent a class session studying newspaper and television advertisements. They concluded that,

> The woman is usually portrayed as a housewife who cleans, cooks and does the laundry. Sometines the man's inability to really clean house is shown. His duties are to play leading roles and adventurous scenes... Advertisements usually appeal to the woman's wish to please her partner...

Other groups agreed that

> [Advertising] tends to stereotype people and to create false images –the macho Marlboro man, the pretty but dumb housewife who needs a man to tell her how to clean the sink.
>
> *(United States of America)*

> Women are turned into consumer goods in a variety of ways... Through advertising, "men only" magazines, beauty contests, etc., women are presented as desirable objects... songs, operas, comic strips, commercial advertising and women's magazines are

> important channels for assigning women to the culturally accepted roles... We should vehemently denounce the mass media for the way they impose an identity on women.
>
> *(Latin American Regional Report)*

Male and female roles

In addition to distinguishing between masculine and feminine characteristics and assigning different values to male and female, most, if not all, cultures have also assigned social roles on the basis of biological gender. One report summed up the situation this way:

> Most societies seem to have prescribed clear social roles based on sexual differentiation. Sometimes the tasks and duties of these roles have been impressed on individuals by various sanctions, including religious ones... Thus it seemed to most Western peoples part of an unchanging order of things that the role of the man was that of hunter, or worker in the forest or fields, while the woman stayed at home engaged in the tasks of nursing and nurture. It seemed natural therefore that women were, on the whole, excluded from public work and the wielding of political power.
>
> *(Great Britain)*

This report added, perhaps optimistically, that

> these stereotyped social roles have been increasingly rejected as it became clear that human life, for each individual woman or man, contained much more than a single socially determined role which could force their pattern of life experience into unnaturally narrow moulds.

A wider selection of reports reveals that this prescription of social roles on the basis of sexual differentiation is a feature of both Western and non-Western cultures. We find in the group reports overwhelming evidence that woman's primary role has traditionally been associated with motherhood. Her tasks have been of a domestic, nurturing nature, preoccupied with childcare and household responsibilities, centred in the private sphere of home and family. Men on the other hand have had the primary role of acting in the public sphere, outside the home, with responsibility for economic support of the family. The reports show that, throughout the world, although women are increasingly employed outside the home, their primary role is still seen as motherhood.

In Latin America "the maternity myth" is summed up in the traditional proverb *tota mulier in utero* which implies that woman is created solely to be a mother, that she can only achieve self-fulfilment through motherhood and that whatever else she does is subordinate to that.

> Woman's place is in the home where she runs the household and manages the money her husband brings in to keep her and her home. But above all, she is a mother... [Man's] responsibility in the home is to bring in the money. But above all, he is a free agent. *(Latin American Regional Report)*

The same division of roles is reported from more "developed" countries:

> Men still see themselves as the breadwinners and women as the homemakers; the idea of woman's role as being limited to "children, church and kitchen" is still very powerful. *(Scotland)*

> In general this idea is dominating: girls take care, boys earn money. *(Netherlands)*

Several reports linked role differentiation with social class:

> The traditional distribution of work among men and women in the bourgeois society has since the nineteenth century been the following: man has the role of maintenance and other roles in the greater society while woman dominates in the reproductive role and the role of socialization (mother), takes care of the internal production in the family (housewife), and the togetherness and care (the social and expressive function, stroking, caring, mediating, consoling) and is wife and sexual partner. In the working class, however, and in earlier societies women were also taking part in the function of maintenance. *(Sweden)*

> Lower class: man earns, wife cleans or earns as well. Middle class: the idea of emancipation of man and woman towards human being gains ground (with consequently greater freedom in roles). Higher class: Mrs X is known as the wife of Mr X (gains status from the profession of her husband). *(Netherlands)*

Women, employment and education

The greatest change taking place in traditional roles is that more and more women are joining the paid workforce. Reports from a number of developing countries noted that education is a key factor in opening up employment opportunities for women and in changing traditional roles. In these countries it is generally the educated, urban woman who works outside the home. In other places, education enables women to have better jobs and to enjoy more independence. One report described the change which had taken place in one woman's life-time:

> A woman member of the group who has passed 50 years of age says that when she was young families were larger and poorer than they are today. In her house there were eight children and the first two girls were never sent to school because they had to look after their brothers when the mother was absent. Only later did this woman learn to write her name and to read the Bible (because she was the only one who converted to the Protestant faith); the sister remained illiterate. At that time women rarely went to work, but there were many girls who worked as domestics in the homes of the rich people of the nation. Today the situation has changed greatly. Almost everyone, men and women, has gone to elementary school. But the women who have not studied have less independence than those who go to school. *(Italy)*

Another group pointed out that lack of education is

> much more serious for the woman, who, from a young age, begins to have children, and has little else to look forward to: domestic employment, work in factories or other similar jobs with little gratification, or simply prostitution. *(Uruguay)*

If education makes it easier for women to challenge cultural role expectations and to get jobs, economic conditions often make it essential. For some privileged women, paid employment may be a matter of choice, a means of self-fulfilment and personal gratification. But for the majority of working women, as for men, paid employment is a matter of economic need. More and more families require more than one income to improve or even maintain their standard of living. In many cases women are themselves heads of households and sole supporters of families. Other women–e.g., unmarried, widowed or divorced–must support themselves financially.

The group reports indicate that as women increasingly assume the role of paid worker they also experience a new set of problems.

According to the reports, women are generally paid less and given fewer opportunities for advancement than men.

> Women are not in practice treated equally in the work place. Problem issues are: sexual harassment, non-implementation of equal pay for work of equal value, lack of opportunity for advancement, female job ghetto, and married women holding two jobs, career and homemaker. *(Canada)*

Many countries now have legislation to protect women in the work force, but, as a report from Scotland observes, "changes in legislation need to be backed by changes in attitudes before the legislation can become fully effective in human terms".

Women are also frequently denied equal opportunity for employment. Their choice of occupation is restricted and their opportunities for advancement are limited, in spite of equal opportunity in law. Social and cultural attitudes often keep women in "the female job ghetto", jobs which are an extension of women's traditional caring and supportive role. According to a report from Burundi, "Traditional jobs are slotted for women: teaching, nursing, secretarial work".

One group described the situation in the following terms:

> In general, women have less education, occupy a lower rank in jobs, and participate less in organization activities than men do. When it comes to engagements outside the home, less performance is expected of women than of men... Women do not get as many challenging tasks as men do, and they get less encouragement when it comes to taking on new projects, making good use of their education, taking on responsibilities or bringing about initiative for some purpose. *(Norway)*

From another part of the world, a similar picture:

> In general the working woman receives less salary than the man, often for performing the same job. It is more difficult for a woman to find a job because companies want to avoid paying maternity benefits, day-care centres, etc., which are required by law in some countries. Also, many employers ignore the benefits stipulated for women. The domestic employee is a frequent case of exploitation: often she doesn't receive even the minimum wage and works more than twelve hours a day.
> *(Latin American Regional Report)*

The consequences of persistent cultural attitudes towards women are nowhere more obvious than in a problem universally experienced by married women who work outside the home. This is the problem of "the double shift", meaning that these women are not allowed to compromise their traditional primary role of childcare and household maintenance. On the contrary, they are expected to add a secondary role (paid employment) to the primary role of motherhood.

> Generally it is expected that the woman cares for the home. This does not mean that she cannot have a job outside her home, but she is responsible for keeping the house clean, cooking, feeding and clothing the family, taking care of the children, etc. *(Denmark)*

> And here we have the major problem of Uruguayan women today: to live in distress because she cannot accomplish efficiently both her jobs, that inside and that outside the house. *(Uruguay)*

> Nowadays, especially in towns, women who are educated go to work outside their homes... in order to enable them to prepare a brighter future for their children, to help their family, and then only perhaps to help their country... As the woman is expected to do both well, housework and work outside, she feels hard pressed. Whilst the man feels that he has completed his duty for the day, the woman has to plan very carefully in order to manage, or to employ a helper in the house. *(Sudan)*

According to one group, this situation reveals a great injustice based on the myth "that housework is by definition the women's job". But, the report declared,

> There is no biological reason that we can see to prevent men from doing all the chores that society has determined as domestic. Women have proved themselves capable of becoming efficient members of the labour force outside the home. The injustice lies in the fact that if she chooses, or for financial reasons is compelled to work outside the home, she is still left with the domestic chores to do after she has finished her day's work.
>
> *(Latin American Regional Report)*

A report from Cuba described an alternative model of development for a Latin American country, one based on a socialist system rather than a "dependent capitalist" system. Since the revolution in Cuba, there have been deliberate efforts to change the economic and social conditions of women. These efforts include the "Family Code" (1975) which states that the work of the home is not the exclusive responsibility of women. But despite this legislation,

> there is still much *machismo* which makes men (not to say women) believe that those who share the traditional tasks of the home are necessarily effeminate or homosexual or men with weak characters who allow themselves to be ruled by their wives. *(Cuba)*

A number of groups reported that traditional attitudes are gradually changing, and that young people in particular are striving to achieve more equal roles within marriage and at work. But this is not always an easy process. One group from the USA commented that it is easier "to accept women in new roles than to accept men in women's roles both in the family and at work". Women frequently feel guilty, torn between home/family and career/work; men often find it difficult to share parental/household responsibilities, rather than merely "helping". Some group members wrote movingly of their personal difficulties in attempting to change traditional roles.

> Dilemma
>
> I scent my baby's soft head:
> two small hands are reaching for mama.
> The students' papers are calling from the desk:
> You promised to have them ready by tomorrow!
> My four-year-old is screaming outside:
> My bike has a flat tire!
> Daddy is late, tired and thinking about the article he is going to write tonight.
> "God, create in me a pure heart!"
>
> My responsibilities within and outside the home are often conflicting: I feel that I am neither a good professional worker nor a good mother and housewife. My husband does not experience the conflict the same way as I do, and sometimes I feel this to be unjust: he is considered to be a very good father because he takes more part in childcare than what is usual in the average family up till now, and he is very successful in his career. This does not mean that he does not face a similar dilemma. But he probably feels more than I do that he has sacrificed something when he cuts down his leisure activities to stay at home. It is he who then is the kind and helping person, while I am the one who constantly

> demands of him that he share in household duties and in caring for the children in order for me to have some time on my own. Truly not a pleasant part to play! *(Norway)*

Men also feel the anguish of new roles and changing identities.

> After the radical treatment of "separation", we try, according to the new rules of the game, to live the "household game". The future will show how successful we are in living with the contradictory expectations and hopes. Certainly new "treatments" will be necessary because changes are not a one-time thing, but need time, patience, courage and tenacity. Sometimes I have no time, no patience, no courage, no tenacity–yes, sometimes I would like to be "normal", i.e., a man who conforms to the norms and expectations. Still, I cannot do this, because I would like to try to liberate myself from the old image of men. But it is very difficult to be and to become a different man. But one thing is sure: I remain a man. *(FRG)*

Women who choose not to work outside the home are also facing a new set of emotional problems. While some women feel guilty because they do not fulfill the traditional duties at home,

> Others feel guilty because they enjoy being a homemaker in these days... We must continue to discredit the fallacy that a woman in rearing a family at home is not making a social contribution. Sometimes a homemaker denigrates herself by saying, "I am just a housewife". *(USA)*

Housework, several groups pointed out, has no exchange value in the economy and so both the work and those who perform it are devalued. One group suggested that it is time "to demythologize the 'ethos of work'", and that "identity is too much associated with having a job" (Netherlands). Another argued that "It must be clearly and forcefully stated that a human person is something more and something other than his or her profession, work or function in society". *(USA)*

Identity of single people

There is considerable unanimity in the group reports that the identity of single people is more problematic than that of those who are married; this is particularly true for single women. The designation "single" includes never-married, divorced and widowed people, but it is the identity of those who have never married which is least well established. This is closely linked with childlessness, again particularly for women. Conventionally, marriage and motherhood go together. It is, of course, possible to be a childless wife or an unmarried mother, but "wife and mother" remains the norm for women in most of the world, thus linking a woman's identity firmly with her biology. And by extension, if "womanhood" or "femininity" is linked with the ability to bear children, the woman who does not do so is considered to be less of a woman.

The identity of single, childless people is most problematic in Asia and Africa where the existence of unmarried women is a new social phenomenon.

> Single women are not recognized as having a proper status in Indian society as everything centres around marriage for women. *(India)*

> [Traditionally] there is no such thing as women remaining unmarried, childless. *(Nigeria)*

> A married woman is more respected than a single one, because she is a mother and has a man as her guard. Married men are also more respected... It is still very hard to have an unmarried son or daughter. *(Gambia)*

In western countries, divorce is becoming more common and people are increasingly choosing a single life, although this does not necessarily mean that they are sexually inactive. In these countries there is the relatively new phenomenon of women and men who are single but not celibate, and who may also choose to have children. For the majority, however, marriage and children is still the acceptable pattern.

In the USA many groups found that while it was not always true that married women are more respected than single women, it was often the case that women with children were held in higher esteem than women without. One group analyzed the situation this way:

> Women are told that in return for passivity, submissiveness, selflessness, lack of ambition, nurturing of others, they are spared the burdens of power, accomplishment and creativity, because they have already been given the greatest creativity of all–mother-

> hood... For those women incapable of or not choosing motherhood, the implication of unworthiness is clear–they must justify themselves as people through biology rather than spirit.

Other groups reported that single women may experience legal discrimination (particularly in obtaining credit facilities and housing), loneliness and social isolation. They may be regarded as pitiable failures or as threats to married stability, and they may be suspected of selfishness or sexual abnormality. The woman who is unmarried and/or childless, whether by chance or by choice, is still considered to be "inferior".

Some different emphases

In their answers to the questions on identity, participants in the Community Study groups expressed considerable agreement about what it means to live as a woman or a man in today's world. However, reports from different parts of the world also reveal some interesting differences in experience, understanding and attitudes.

In the Middle East reports there is generally more concern with maintaining and affirming the differences between women and men. One woman at the Middle East regional meeting stated that

> The 20th century brought with it a dangerous trend that deprives woman of her femininity and man of his manliness, and it is prevalent among today's youth. It is the result of non-acceptance by some girls of their sex. Naturally, this gave girls an inferiority complex which erupted in the form of a desire to imitate and resemble man. *(Middle East Regional Report)*

On the other hand, the report also acknowledged that women are not treated equally in society:

> A woman has her own personality in our culture, but she is not always respected. We are at the stage of the Middle Ages in our outlook towards women. Maybe we have not arrived at a stage where a woman can be seen as having a clear personality. The liberation of woman is also the liberation of society.

The question from the Middle East appears to be how to give women and men equality in society, while still affirming the essential difference between the two sexes.

In India, women have constitutional equality in law but this has yet to be fully realized in life. For example, the system of marriage, divorce and dowry payment reflects an inequality in the valuation of women and men. In addition, Indian society is strongly influenced by class and caste. The relationship between women of different class/caste backgrounds is highly restricted. The affluent, educated women of the upper classes/castes do not reflect the situation of the majority of Indian women who, in the words of one report, bear the burden of "oppressive ideals which keep women within four walls like a parrot in the cage".

Reports from both India and Africa stated that recent history has witnessed a decline in the status of women. In Africa, this was attributed to the influence of outside forces, particularly in colonial times.

> In matriarchal societies, women were heads of their families, but with the advent of colonialism, Islam and Christianity, women became relegated to an inferior position... It is painful to the essence of African womanhood that a woman, whose female ancestors were very dynamically involved in every aspect of human life, now defines herself in terms of irrelevance and impotence. *(Africa Regional Report)*

> Despite the historic traditions of our country and the exalted role of women in our society before colonization, the colonizers and Madagascan collaborators tried to wipe out the indigenous civilization and replace it with a white civilization, western in general and French in particular. Especially as far as the woman was concerned, this was a patent regression–the French woman had not even the right to vote while the Madagascan woman, prior to this [colonization] had already been participating in the political life of their country... *(Madagascar)*

It must be added, however, that African traditions are also not wholly favourable to women. Mention was made in several reports of taboos (e.g. menstruation taboos) being used against women.

It is clear from a number of comments in reports from the Middle East, Asia and Africa that the identity of women in the extended family (the common family unit in these areas) is different in some respects from that of women in the nuclear family (common in western countries). For example, in the extended family the role of daughter-in-law has a quite different significance. Some suggested that this is a subject for further research.

In Latin America the question of identity is seen as rooted in the problems of an unjust society. Women in Latin America live in a society dominated by "machismo", an ideology of male superiority. Latin American women are also very conscious of the oppression of social class which means that women often suffer the double oppression of class and sex. Some even experience multiple oppression because of their race or social/political condition. At the Latin American regional meeting participants stated:

1. We start from the fact that in our society we cannot talk about "woman" in generic terms because women belong to different classes, and for this reason they enter into conflict not only with society's male supremacy structures, but also with women and men of other classes.
2. We purposely focus our discussion from the viewpoint of the doubly-oppressed woman, that is, the woman who on the one hand belongs to the exploited class, and on the other hand has been further marginalized because of her sex.
3. We believe that women are engaged in two related and simultaneous struggles: the struggle for existence within the exploited classes and the struggle for their rights as women.
4. We are conscious of the fact that the real fulfilment of all women as active agents in society will only be achieved when it is accompanied by a radical change in economic, social and political structures, a change oriented toward building a new society, where new women and men will share life together.

(Latin American Regional Report)

This report also refers to the very difficult situation of women in countries governed by military regimes, where women suffer "not only scarcity of provisions, but also repression, persecution, rape, torture, imprisonment, the pain of losing a loved one, or death itself".

In the Caribbean there is a struggle to achieve a sense of national identity, a struggle to avoid being swamped by North American culture. Groups in the Middle East, Asia and Africa were also concerned to preserve their cultural identity in the face of massive western influences. For this reason some felt uneasy about questioning the traditional cultural identity of women.

The most rapid and pronounced changes in the roles of women and men have occurred in the more industrialized, western countries;

yet the reports show that laws and regulations are often more advanced than social attitudes, and that traditional stereotypes of male and female identity and roles are still influential.

For many women in these parts of the world, the major problem is how to reconcile and combine the two roles of paid worker and mother.

> Our problem is not equality as such, but rather, how to reconcile professional life and motherhood. Responsible jobs make demands on the whole person, but so does motherhood, so that for us the question is: "How much do we like being mothers?" Every family tries to solve this problem as best it can. *(FRG)*

In socialist countries where there is legislation for equality and where women are fully integrated into the paid work force, there are still difficulties in changing attitudes.

> In fact, the images of men and women are not characterized only by new, socialist norms and the struggle to implement them. They are also determined to varying degrees by traditional and at present contradictory elements which originate in different areas and various historical periods of our society. They are observable in the images of women and men and in the relationships between them, in spite of the widespread similarity in lifestyles, varying historical developments and variations due to antecedents and income. *(GDR)*

In Scandinavian countries, perhaps more than anywhere else, there has been a real effort to promote equality of the sexes; but in general the result has been that "women have been made masculine in a higher degree than men have been made feminine" (Sweden). Now there is a greater concern with developing humanity:

> The equality thinking started out of too many features of the living patterns of man ("to become like man"; "to get the rights which man has now"), instead of finding new models for acting like human beings. *(Finland)*

Reports from western countries generally lay more stress than do those from other regions on the rights of the individual to personal fulfilment, and are also more concerned with the identity and roles of men. A number of groups pointed out that men also suffer from stereotyping and rigid role definitions. While men may be dominant in many areas of life, they are generally regarded as inferior to women in the emotional sphere.

> Compared with women, man is unequal on the emotional level. Education and role expectations make it difficult for him to fully express himself–he has less possibilities for tenderness, affection, uncertainty and positive giving up. *(Finland)*

One group reported a "classic exchange" illustrating this difference between women and men:

> Woman: How do you feel now?
> Man: About my feelings? I'd have to think. *(Australia)*

Some groups observed that men may feel trapped by their work, by the need to earn a living and to support a family, while at the same time spending the greater part of their time away from the family. Those who seek to change their role often face difficulties, particularly in social attitudes which categorize them as "unmasculine" or "effeminate". For men, as for women, the question is how to live as authentic human beings.

> It is clear that men have trouble finding their new role. Women should take part in the thinking about this change and take some of the responsibility for it. In this process one should emphasize those aspects which are "profitable" for men: e.g., the right to have and to express feelings, a matter-of-fact acceptance and independence in carrying out responsibilities and duties in the home and family, friendships with women on the basis of equal partnership. *(GDR)*

Responses from Orthodox Christians emphasized that there are profound and permanent differences between women and men. The basis for this distinction was understood to be principally theological and spiritual.

> The differences between women and men remain forever, even in the kingdom of God, both physically and spiritually... *(USA)*

> When one takes account of the only psychological data observable, the differences between men and women seem less clear. The social roles are increasingly interchangeable... The ideal man or the ideal woman is in large part the product of history and culture. Is this to say that over above social psychology no more

> profound and universal archetypal configuration corresponds to them in the human psyche? The Orthodox Christian will say that he discovers in Christ and in the Virgin Mary the revelation of the eternal archetypes. *(France)*

According to Orthodox tradition and teaching,

> ...while Jesus is generally the model and pattern of all human perfection, and while Mary is the person who has accomplished divine perfection most fully, Jesus is still specifically a man, and Mary specifically a woman. This means not only that we contemplate the model of human perfection in a male form, and its perfect realization in a female form; it means as well that there is a sense in which Jesus is also the perfect example for men, as the Virgin Mary is for women... It is claimed that Jesus realizes the general Christian virtues in a particularly masculine form, while Mary actualizes them in a particularly feminine form. The sexual distinctions and images of Jesus and Mary endure everlastingly... *(USA)*

Orthodox responses focused largely on the question of women's identity in the church. Concerning the question of identity in society, they generally accepted the principle of equality between women and men, but made few comments about their actual experiences.

> Orthodox Christians seem to agree generally that there are no secular professions which in themselves exclude women; except, of course, those which also exclude men because they are evil. And most will agree that there are certain professions in such areas as those dealing with education and healing and welfare, where a woman can be more effective than a man because of the specifically feminine expression of her human qualities. Whatever a woman's profession, however, all would agree that in the Orthodox view women having the same jobs and professions as men should have the same wages and benefits, and the same opportunities for promotion and advancement. This is simply a matter of justice. *(USA)*

In the Middle East there seemed to be less acceptance of the idea of Orthodox women working outside the home, an attitude shared by other Christians in that region. One participant at the regional meeting exclaimed,

> Today woman is demanding her rights. Has not God granted her rights that exceed those she is demanding? Is she not mistress of her home? Through her femininity she can attain all that she wishes, so what need has she today to leave her home and work outside its bounds? Housekeeping is in itself an independent management and requires a lot of time and saves a lot of money. Woman complements man, but she does not replace him, and if she does, what need would she have for him?
>
> *(Middle East Regional Report)*

For Orthodox Christians both celibacy and marriage are possible life-styles; but, although consecrated celibacy is accepted and honoured, all Orthodox responses indicated the primary importance of woman's role in the family, and the unacceptability of social changes which threaten the institutions of marriage and family.

> The "liberation" of women, and their massive entry into "public life", has led to a radical alteration of family life and, in many cases, to its ideological rejection and factual decomposition. This is the most critical issue for Orthodox Christians since, in the Orthodox view, the family is not simply the "traditional form" of human community, but it is the basic and essential form of human being and life as created by God in his own image and likeness. The family is a "small church", a creaturely reflection of the Holy Trinity itself. It is sacramentally constituted as an expression and realization of the Kingdom of God on earth. The existence of the family is not a debatable issue for Orthodox Christians. *(USA)*

IDENTITY IN THE CHURCH

According to the Community Study group reports, women generally experience their identity in society as that of "second-class" human beings, inferior and subordinate to men. But how do women experience their identity in the church, or rather in the many different churches represented in the Community Study? Much of the material in the group reports relates to this question and, as one would expect, there are differences of doctrine and of practice. Yet, in spite of the differences, once again a remarkably consistent picture emerges from the reports.

Theory and practice in the churches

The reports make clear that in matters concerning women and men the churches are greatly influenced by social and cultural attitudes. Frequently the churches are experienced as perpetuating or endorsing these attitudes and the consequent sex-role stereotyping, sometimes to a much greater extent than in society where fairly rapid changes may be taking place.

> Our Christian churches... have frequently permitted the same conditions of injustice which exist in our society to seep into church structures themselves. *(Latin American Regional Report)*

> The church is always lagging behind society when it comes to women/men relationships. The church itself practises oppression so how can the church have the effrontery to correct the society when it is also oppressive? *(African Regional Report)*

> The church supports the role society has assigned to women and gives it religious sanction. *(Asian Regional Report)*

> It is in the church that we often come up against the most rigid stereotyping. *(Great Britain)*

> It was clearly shown that reforms take place more slowly in the church than in society. Equally, churches are more apt to apply different rules in judging behaviour, according to whether a man or a woman is involved. *(FRG)*

Most of the study groups concentrated more on the actual experience of women and men within the churches than on official teaching and pronouncements. They looked at the roles and functions undertaken by women and by men, and, in their conclusions, most agreed that "in various ways women experience differentiation in treatment because of their sex" (Norway). They reported that women frequently far outnumber men in church membership and attendance at worship, but their participation is often limited to certain activities closely related to women's traditional social roles. This means that, in general, women have little part in decision-making or positions of responsibility in the churches. In the words of one typical report:

> Women are engaged in jobs like caring for children, being members of social committees (serving at tables), carrying out secretarial duties in committees, relief work in the congregation –

> in short, jobs similar to those ranging within the traditional role of women in the home. Men most often carry duties as leaders, are active speakers etc.–tasks that are of higher prestige and esteem than the traditional female occupations. *(Norway)*

A number of Protestant groups in West Germany and Switzerland summarized their findings by pointing out that,

> Although the churches in both countries formally grant women full legal rights of participation at all levels, church life is still divided into public and private spheres. Men dominate the public area as pastors, synod and council members. Women dominate the private world of the congregational life of local parishes.

The picture is much the same in other parts of the world, especially those with a western culture.

> In principle, church structures are supposed to be open, but they have a strong tendency to be patriarchal. Women make up the majority of church workers, but they are mostly in minor positions. This fact is most clearly demonstrated in the composition of congregational life: women, who are to listen, are at the bottom and the few men who have the say are at the top. *(GDR)*

> Legally and in theory, opportunities in church and society are equal for men and women. In practice, a male dominant tradition is widely accepted by both men and (many) women... "Men make decisions and women make tea...." The talents and contributions that individuals bring to the life of the congregation are still forced into stereotyped moulds of expression or organization. *(Scotland)*

> Within most church structures, women have, at least in theory, the opportunity to participate on equal terms with men.... However, in practice women are poorly represented at all levels of decision-making while they have almost sole responsibility for such duties as childminding, cleaning and providing food and drink. *(New Zealand)*

> Too often women are the "folding chairs": the church needs them when men have less time or interest. *(Netherlands)*

> The word "service" is frequently used in the churches. It is almost always applied to women; it is an extension of the role of mother and housewife; it perpetuates an image dear to society: "woman as ornament". *(Switzerland)*

Men dominate in other areas too, such as theological education. One group of seminary students wrote that,

> The given system of theological education is set up for the training of single young male students:
> - no female faculty person,
> - professors rarely recommend, never require the reading of, works by women scholars,
> - women students regarded as freaks,
> - no feminine perspective in how to do theology. *(USA)*

Open and deliberate discrimination against women may be rare and contrary to official church policy, and yet the fact remains that in male-dominated churches women are often "invisible".

> The causing of women to be "invisible" occurs in various ways: men's world, their experiences, interests and activities are considered to be important (by men in the church), while one "forgets", does not observe, or does not consider as important the affairs and activities in which women are engaged. Contents of theological work, of sermons and of programmes during conferences indicate this. *(Norway)*

Even if largely restricted to "service" roles, women are active in church life at the congregational level. In fact, a number of groups reported that in congregational and parish life women and men participated equally, although this generally means that women share men's traditional roles and responsibilities rather than that men assume "women's roles". One group noted that,

> There are few men teaching, particularly young children, or performing any support services like providing food for functions or cleaning up afterwards. *(USA)*

At higher levels of decision-making and church government, where "more important" decisions are made and where more real power exists, women are greatly under-represented in most churches. Several groups provided figures to illustrate this under-representation.

> Seventy percent of active members of the dominant church are women, but the percentage of women in governing bodies of the church diminishes in proportion to the real power of that body,

i. e., forty percent of women on parish boards, only about eighteen percent in the National Church Assembly. *(Finland)*

On an average, women make up 80%-90% of all church-goers. There are many more women's organizations in the congregation than men's organizations. The percentage of women on local church boards is relatively high: on an average, about 50 per cent. The reason for this is that men, for whatever reasons, are not willing to take leading positions in local congregations. The percentage of women at the next level of leadership is significantly lower: 14% to 18% on church boards at district levels, between 20% and 0% at the Synod level, according to the percentage of women on the local church board. *(GRD)*

A different situation prevails in the Roman Catholic Church since Roman Catholic women are excluded by canon law from certain forms of participation. According to one group, this exclusion means for the most part:

- that women cannot be ordained (Can. 968);
- that women cannot preside at the eucharist (Can. 709,2);
- that women cannot be empowered with ecclesiastical jurisdiction (Can. 118);
- that congregations of women are always dependent on a man.

(France)

Several French groups pointed out, however, that this legal exclusion of women is not necessarily accepted in the daily life of the Roman Catholic Church, at least in their country.

While the texts concerning women and those which define their "rights" and their "functions" have not been modified, the exigencies of daily church life have led them to assume more numerous and more important responsibilities in various communities, where, with rare exceptions, they are now accepted and recognized. Women in fact carry out many functions, for example,

1) they transmit the gospel by the spoken word;
2) they exercise liturgical functions;
3) they exercise pastoral functions, even though these rarely have official character or are given any recognition by the Catholic hierarchy. *(France)*

In Asian, African and Latin American countries, where cultural attitudes regarding women are often more restrictive than in Europe and North America, these restrictions are reflected in church practices and teachings. In churches in some countries, women are not equal even in theory.

In Latin America *machismo* is a powerful influence in church as well as in society.

> Inserted in a society in which women are marginalized and subjected, our churches have excluded women from their own structures, assigning them tasks with the roles traditionally conceived as feminine (cleaning and decorating the church, cooking, Sunday School teaching, etc.)... denying women the possibility of participating actively in tasks such as theology. These structures, based on a male-centred ideology, leave no room for a new relationship of liberty or full companionship. They simply perpetuate the roles which society assigns to women and men. *(Latin American Regional Report)*

A Caribbean report notes that

> In church circles women are, in effect, kept out of church leadership. There is real need for both men and women to recognize women's potential for leadership. In spite of their numerical superiority, women continue–by and large–to do the "donkey work" and to vote the few available men into office. *(Jamaica)*

In Asia women often struggle against discrimination which results from cultural attitudes supported by the churches. Members of one Indian church reported that

> Equality between women and men is accepted in principle but in ritualistic practices women are considered secondary, inferior and less holy. For example, at holy communion men are served first, in baptism male babies or adults are baptised first, and in the marriage ceremony the prayers and blessings for the bridegroom are said before those of the bride. *(Asian Regional Report)*

A Korean group wrote poignantly that

> Some denominations do not allow women to approach the pulpit. No women can stand on the pulpit. No women pray at Sunday worship service. No women preach sermons on Sunday morning

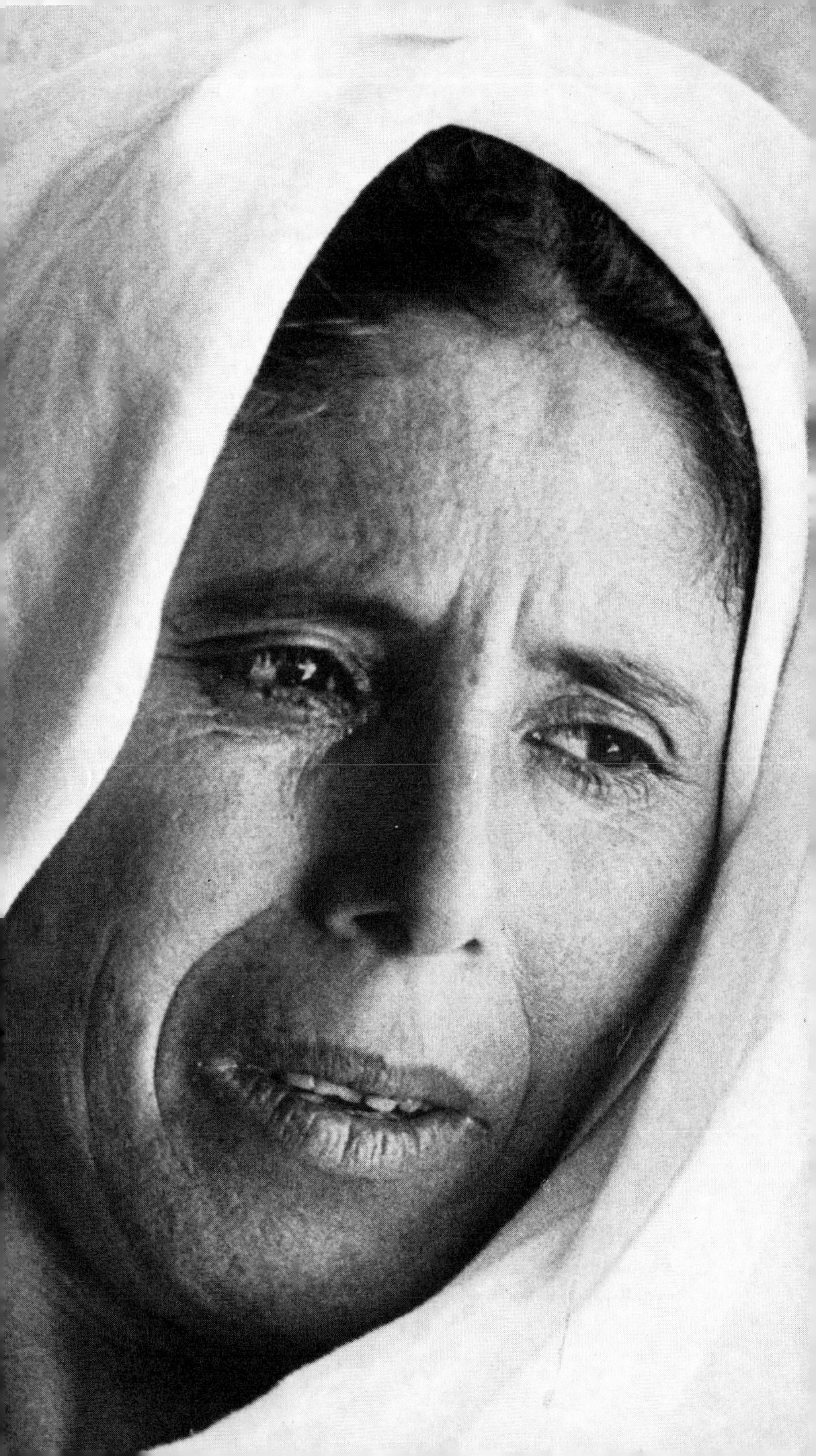

> service. No woman minister, not even an elder.... Bible teaches us to help the outsiders. We feel we are also outsiders from men's world. *(Korea)*

Another group reported that in Indonesia 70-90 percent of churchgoers are women but that there is a very small number of women theologians, Bible teachers, or deaconesses. The church is reluctant to accept women as preachers or as teachers at the theological institutes.

In Africa, cultural attitudes, combined with missionary teaching, frequently limit women's participation in the churches. The reports seem to indicate, however, that, on the whole, African women are more ready to accept a certain division of labour within the church. Women leaders of the Sudan Council of Churches wrote:

> Women feel that they work hand in hand with men. They visit people in their homes, clean churches, care for children, and they like to do these. Women are leaders in women's groups, they are deacons, but not yet pastors or bishops. Women are the believers, mothers, based in the family, an example to youth. Men work in the outside world, spreading the faith. *(Sudan)*

According to another report,

> Women are by far a majority in the church. They are also the most active in the church, because by tradition the family and religion (thus the church for Christians) are the privileged areas of activity for women. It is often they who, along with the pastor, visit the sick, represent the congregation at burials or make the traditional visit to the bereaved, etc. But they are also most often the silent majority in the church, applying to the letter the recommendations of St Paul to the Corinthians. *(Madagascar)*

Active discrimination does exist in some areas.

> In some African cultures, still today, women are not allowed to sit among the men in the church. The women can give witness, but they are not allowed to participate in decision-making. *(African Regional Report)*

> In our society, a woman can be a Senator in the House of Assembly but may not be allowed to teach anyone else but children in her church. Generally as the society regards women as

> weak vessels so does the church except in cases where one or two women in the church are ranked among the elders either because they are founding members, they are very wealthy and contribute huge amounts to the purse of the church, or they are very old. *(Nigeria)*

In Orthodox churches, "women and men are called by God to all of the various ministries and services in the church, except episcopacy and presbyterate" (USA) and, in principle, "the church must recognize the person who is gifted to serve it better, without discrimination on the basis of sex" (Middle East Regional Report). But in practice some division of roles on the basis of sex remains quite common. According to one participant at the Middle East Regional Consultation,

> In the church, woman has her own field of work and man has another. Above all, she is an educator because she understands the child intuitively and she is near to him. Her role is extremely important in Christian teaching and education, in supporting the oppressed and enlightening the illiterate women, in planting faith where there is none, in helping the doctor in his work and carrying out social work.

A French group gave a full account of participation by women in their Orthodox parish:

> The women participate actively in the life of the church. They can be elected members of the local church board, which they often preside jointly with the priest who is the rector of the congregation. They sing in the choir, act as "readers" and take over the religious education of the children and adolescents. Some women take courses in theology.... Nothing prevents a woman from "doing theology", even outside of the academic sphere. *(France)*

But this group also questioned whether this degree of women's participation was satisfactory:

> Women take care of many tasks, but in the execution rather than in the conception of such tasks. Are we willing enough to solicit their creativity in the sphere of thinking, of faith or of spirituality? Are we willing to have them participate, as part of the whole people of God, in positions of responsibility and in decision-making, if only as lay people? *(France)*

One issue raised by the Community Study that has generated considerable controversy in the churches is the ordination of women. This is not the place to deal with this topic in depth; a Community Study consultation was held to discuss women's ordination in 1979 and the results have been published in the *Ordination of Women in Ecumenical Perspective: Workbook for the Churches' Future* (edited by C. Parvey, Geneva, 1980). But several groups pointed out that the discussion of ordination is intimately and inevitably connected with the questions of identity. Even in those churches that do ordain women, the role of minister is sometimes seen as incompatible with traditional understandings of what it means to be female. At the African Regional Consultation, an ordained woman from Uganda reported:

> I was the first black woman pastor in an urban church. When I started working and going into the homes, the women would not accept me. They looked at me as "too pushy", they felt I had gone too far.

According to another:

> You put on the clerical collar, then the feminine image is spoiled. That's what people think. They ask, "Who will marry you?" There is still this patronizing attitude towards women.
>
> *(African Regional Report)*

Elsewhere groups found that the assignments given to women clergy often conform to the traditional stereotypes.

> In most Protestant churches all forms of ministry are open to women and men but there is a tendency that the higher in the church hierarchy the fewer women you see and they encounter more difficulties. There is also a tendency for women ministers to work in special areas associated with traditional role patterns, e.g. teaching young children, hospital and old age pastorates.
>
> *(Netherlands)*

Towards new ways of participation

In spite of regional and denominational differences, it is clear from the reports that women and men generally participate in the churches in much the same way as they do in secular society. Women and men do different things and fulfill different roles, based not simply on individual gifts and interests but on gender. Some groups noted that this situation is changing, that women now have more rights, responsibilities and opportunities than in the past, but these changes are usually the result of changing conditions and attitudes in society. The churches in other words, tend to follow society rather than to lead it.

> The church does not support the viewpoint that women are inferior to men. On the other hand it does not do anything to promote the equalizing of men and women in the society or in the church. *(Denmark)*

> The church takes no systematic actions in order to prevent discrimination against women or in order to support increased equality. *(Sweden)*

Some thought that the churches should be more active in initiating changes both in their own structures and in society.

> There was a feeling that the church, rather than merely reflecting a concern whose initiative appears to have been secular, should rather take the reins and lead the way, and make bolder declarations on behalf of equal treatment and regard under the Christian faith, so that such a vision can shape and mould a future that is far more ethical and God-like than the past from which we have so far been acting. *(USA)*

Others expressed a reluctance to follow traditional male patterns, a desire to seek new, more human ways of acting and relating.

> One must create, invent new relationships in order to escape from fixed patterns, to go from a relationship of rivalry to one of co-operation, which presupposes the recognition of our richness and our poverty. *(Switzerland)*

> In order to be recognized, women must prove that they are the equals of men on their own territory or that they can supplant them, an attitude that seems to lead to an impasse. Isn't there something better to do than to reproduce a society and a church such as we have today? Is there not a feminine voice to discover and to promote? Would not humanity be enriched by a new approach to the problems, a new vision of the world, if women could bring their own values to bear by participating in the centres of power? *(France)*

Traditional structures of authority were particularly questioned. There were many suggestions from the groups that women, because of their life-experience of powerlessness, might be able to develop new, non–hierarchical forms of authority. In the words of one report,

> Just to ordain women to ministry and eldership or even to set up democratic groups for some lay participation is not enough, for this is only to tinker with a situation where all too often the structures of the church reflect exactly those of the world. Authority and power in the church are still male-shaped and male-dominated... If the church is to show to the world the kind of authority that is characteristic of the Christ of the New Testament and the kind of power that exists by the operation of the Holy Spirit in the lives of those who in the world's terms are weak and without might, then it has to begin to develop a life-style that will proclaim the liberating action of God. In this development the place of women is central and crucial. *(Scotland)*

Despite some signs of change, some willingness to hear what women are saying about their identity and participation in the churches, progress is slow and many women participants in the Community Study expressed "a growing experience of frustration through lack of acceptance" (England), and a degree of anger or disillusion with the church for being "a repressive institution which fails to live up to its own ideals" (New Zealand).

Groups also acknowledged that women are often slow to take advantage of existing opportunities for fuller participation. Many commented on women's lack of self-confidence, their reluctance to step out of traditional role patterns, their acceptance of imposed limitations. Two groups summed up the situation succinctly:

> Women still think poorly of themselves. *(Sudan)*

> Women still have a real feeling of inferiority and there is an absence of solidarity among themselves and in their judgments about each other. *(Belgium)*

It is hardly surprising that women are often handicapped by this belief in their own inferiority, for the church and society have both taught them in many ways, directly and indirectly, that they are inferior. As one group put it,

> It takes courage and pain to break through to who you are when the culture and church have defined who you *ought to be*. *(Australia)*

Language and imagery

A number of study groups commented on the way in which traditional language and imagery have helped to reinforce belief in the inferiority of women and subtly to exclude them from full participation in the human community and in the church. There is a growing understanding that language shapes thought and experience just as much as thought and experience shape language. All language about God is necessarily inadequate, but today more and more people are questioning the particular inadequacy of the traditional use of predominantly masculine words to describe and address God. (This problem is explored in depth in Part III of this volume: "Towards a Theology of Human Wholeness".) It was pointed out in a number of group reports that the use of almost exclusively masculine terms and images to describe God makes it difficult for women to claim their identity in terms of being made "in the image of God".

> It affects and diminishes their understanding of themselves, and can make them feel diminished by others. *(England)*

The concept of God as "father" was particularly questioned by several groups.

> We are reminded that when "Father God" calls "Mother Church" into being it appears that a sex-bound hierarchy is set up. Only a man can be "papa", "father", the pope, the priest, while women are only called into subservient roles... Objections could be raised at every instance in which man's "fathering" is seen as superior to woman's "mothering". Women are robbed of the opportunity to lead, to participate in the creative "fathering" of God. *(USA)*

> God, Master, Almighty, emphasizes the distance. Our images are more human. Why can't we say Mother? *(FRG)*

To think of God as "mother" was revolutionary for some in the Community Study.

> We used to imagine God with male imagery. We were taught to call God father. We need to change man-made language. Now we understand we can imagine God with female imagery. Reading Isaiah 49:14-18 we were so amazed to find these words in the Bible. Nobody had ever told us to imagine God as a loving

> mother. Thinking of God who has engraved my name on the palm of God's hands makes us feel so much closer to God, just like to our own mother. It makes it easier to understand God. We have our own children. We love them very much. I can forgive them again and again. I do not want them to suffer. I only want them to be happy. How wonderful to think of God as a mother. How come we have never paid any attention to the Bible verses about a hen caring for her chickens? When we had read the same verses before, it had never struck us that God could be a mother. Now we know so many verses about God's image as a loving mother. When we were reading these verses we cried, "Amen, Halleluja!" *(Korea)*

> When I first heard "she" used in relation to God, I felt that this was irreverent. Then I realized that this was really a reflection of my feelings about myself. When I truly believed that I was made in the image of God, I had no more problems with God as "she". It was a salvation experience. *(Australia)*

> To question the language about God is a sensitive area for many Christians. Some find the suggestion of change puzzling, threatening, and even offensive. Others see language as crucially important, arguing that "belief in the inferiority of women has surely been reinforced in many minds by the familiar masculine language" in which "the image of God as father is so strong that God is naturally seen as a male". *(USA)*

The language used to speak to and of the people of God may also be dominated by masculine terminology. In the words of one report,

> Prayers, hymns and sermons are all generally couched in language which suggests that all those present in the church are men–which is usually far from the case. *(England)*

This report continues,

> For the women in the congregation to hear regularly the phrase in the Creed which says Christ died "for us men and for our salvation", to be invited to sing "Rise up, O men of God", or to find themselves addressed as "Brother", is needlessly misleading and inappropriate, and can indeed be humiliating. The words which are used of God's people should surely be inclusive, not exclusive.

Another group looked specifically at the question of sexism in the language of ecclesial texts, examining a hymn book, the church constitution, a church leaders' manual, and a leading church newspaper.

> We were especially interested to know if our ideas about the church as a community of men and women with equal rights is reflected in the language. Or is the still widespread hierarchical structure of our church reflected in the language? *(FRG)*

The group found that predominantly masculine language was used, but that attempts were being made for more inclusive language. Others, too, reported changes and reviews of language; but for many it remains true that language is simply another means by which women, included as "men" or "brothers", lose their own identity and become "invisible".

Scripture and identity

Participants in the Community Study agreed that the Bible is authoritative for Christian belief, although, as might be expected, they differed in their understandings of the exact nature and weight of this authority. They also held differing views about the interpretation of Scripture. (These issues of scriptural authority and interpretation are dealt with in depth in Part II of this book: "The Authority of Scripture in Light of the New Experiences of Women".) As far as the relationship between Scripture and identity is concerned, the only major difference of opinion was between Orthodox groups and those of other confessional backgrounds. Orthodox reports made clear their belief that the Tradition of the Church, which includes the Scriptures, supplies the answers to questions about women and men, "the basic, essential and final revelation of the truth of God about women and men in the church" (USA).

Protestant and Roman Catholic participants generally took a more questioning, even critical, attitude to the interpretation and use of scripture. They argued that the Bible has traditionally been interpreted by men from a male perspective. Scripture has been used to reinforce cultural sexual stereotyping even as cultural attitudes and beliefs about women have frequently influenced the interpretation of passages relating to women.

> There is a traditional interpretation of the Bible regarding women that tends to marginalize them by asserting that the Bible presents women as inferior to men. *(Latin American Regional Report)*

> The traditional reading of the Bible, and some theology, are influenced by a profound and often unconscious attitude based on the idea of male superiority and dominance... . *(Switzerland)*

> A patriarchal society has interpreted the Bible and established the church with patriarchal interpretations and attitudes. *(Denmark)*

> We discussed much concerning the status and roles of women in church and society through the biblical outlook. It always invited comparison with our traditions as the tradition of Israel and ours are similar–a patriarchal society with women playing a subordinate role. We realized that the biblical message we got was quite often misinterpreted and quoted with bias. *(Indonesia)*

A number of the reports described how biblical passages depicting the inferiority and subordinate status of women were used in church teaching and preaching, while other passages, with a positive view of women, were ignored or neglected. The creation accounts in Genesis and certain Pauline passages were frequently cited as examples of masculine bias in both the original texts and their subsequent interpretation.

> The account of Genesis 1, in which God created the human being, woman and man, has been neglected in favour of the account of Genesis 2, in which God created first the man and then the woman. This overshadows the version in which man and woman together are made in the image of God (Genesis 1) and responsible for creation; on the other hand the fact that in Genesis 2 Eve is created after Adam and is designated a helpmate similar to Adam has been interpreted as a sign of inferiority and of dependence of the woman in relation to the man. And what has not been said on the subject of the famous rib of Adam, from which Eve was drawn...! *(Switzerland)*

> The Genesis account is what Nigerians, including small boys, use as an evidence of inferiority of woman to man. In a primary school a boy and a girl had a quarrel and the boy said, "Come here, if you dare. I will prove to you today that I have nine rib-bones while you have just seven!" *(Nigeria)*

> Woman as temptress in Genesis 3, reflected in 1 Timothy 2: 11-15, seems to have established women's immutable inferiority, not merely physical but also intellectual and moral. The subordi-

> nation of women in Genesis 3:16-19 is not a command but a curse for disturbing the original peace of creation.
>
> *(Asian Regional Report)*

Groups distinguished different strands or tendencies of the biblical message, rejecting what they regarded as time- and culture-bound prescriptions referring to women and emphasizing those strands which present a vision of equality.

> We admit that in the church there exist, or at least still survive, retarding tendencies influenced by superficial understanding of some biblical passages, like for instance Genesis 2, 3 or even 1 Corinthians 7. We discern, however, that the Scriptures are not uniform even in this matter. It is possible to pursue in them an inner struggle for the situation of woman. For instance, already in Genesis 2:24 inside the patriarchal society quite a contradictory element breaks through. *(Czechoslovakia)*

> The central role played by women in the history of the people of Israel was shown using biblical accounts from the story of Moses–an aspect that has largely disappeared due to a male interpretation of history and the hostile attitude that the church has had towards women in the past. *(FRG)*

> We have got to a stage where we do not quote "Slaves, obey your masters" (Ephesians 6:5) and go ahead and have slaves. Yet when it comes to relationships of women and men there are some who quote the creation story and what St. Paul said to take literally the subordinate position of women to men and the prohibition of women speaking or holding authority... . We cannot transcribe what happened in the past to present-day conditions, irrespective of the changing relationships of the present day. *(India)*

A number of groups stressed that the interpretation and application of biblical passages must be done with regard to their historical and sociological context.

> In various passages of the Bible we see women relegated to an inferior level. Consequently, the scriptures have influenced much in past times, and in fact continue to influence today in this matter. However, in our group we considered the importance of the historical social context of the epoch in which the Bible was written. And then we were able to encounter biblical passages

which reinstate women in face of the concepts and ideas of the time in which it was written. We were then able to see women considered on the same level as men before God. *(Uruguay)*

Neither the Old nor the New Testament can be treated as a code book of timeless truths which can be isolated from the situations in which they were uttered. Therefore, in supporting a particular rule in governing behaviour we must not quote texts apart from their context.... We believe that Christians need to emphasize more than we usually do that the earliest witnesses to Christ, whose faith is recorded in what we now call the New Testament, were women and men not only in time but also of their time. The questions they asked are not always the same as ours with regard to sexuality, since the circumstances of their world were not the same as ours. Therefore the conclusions they reached are not always appropriate to our context... . *(England)*

According to Community Study participants,

One must now re-read the Bible and re-discover its feminine dimension. This is an enrichment, because this re-reading expands and deepens the traditional reading. *(Switzerland)*

In this new reading, attempted by many groups, major emphasis was given to the life and teaching of Jesus.

How Jesus acted towards women was revolutionary. Jesus treated woman as whole person. We believe in Jesus and follow him. If the church is to follow the way Jesus taught, the church should not degrade women. *(Korea)*

Jesus lives differently, interacts differently with women from his contemporaries. He changes his "roles" and women thereby also change their "role" because of having met him... . Much of Jesus' behaviour is revolutionary. Firmly grounded structures start to topple. The gospel questions structures, it does not stabilise them. *(GDR)*

Many reports gave an account of the words and actions of Jesus in relation to women. The following quotation is representative:

We observe that Jesus treated the Samaritan woman as a person worthy of his self-disclosure as the Messiah. In this way he demonstrated that in him all contempt and marginalization of women can be overcome (John 4).

> From the beginning of his ministry, and going very much counter to the customs of his society, Jesus included women in his group of followers (Luke 8:1-3). Faithful to the end, these women accompanied him until the moment of his death (Mark 15:40-41; Matthew 27:55-56; Luke 23:49).
>
> Jesus also chose women as the first witnesses of his resurrection and commissioned them to communicate to the others this all-surpassing event, the essential foundation for the establishment of the church (Mark 16:1-11; Matthew 28:1-10; Luke 24:1-11; John 20:1-18). *(Latin American Regional Report)*

Groups also devoted considerable attention to Galatians 3:27-28 as a key text for a proper Christian understanding of identity.

> It was agreed that 1 Corinthians 11 and 14 are often used against women's participation in the church. The question was asked why is Galatians 3:28 not used as a counter-argument? Few people had ever heard a sermon on this subject. It has been more or less ignored by the male-dominated church. This passage which stresses equality in Christ and specifically includes the relationship between women and men is a genuine transmission of the good news. In the relationship of God with us, we are the chosen people, women and men, rich, poor, etc. We are part of God and together with God in Christ. This is the kind of partnership we are meant to have in the church. *(African Regional Report)*

An Orthodox group argued, however, that this passage does not mean that all distinctions between women and men are obliterated. Rather,

> What has been annihilated and destroyed "in Christ" is not the natural distinction between women and men but all division between them with the enmity and hostility which comes from domination, subservience and tyranny which derives not from God but from the devil and sin. *(USA)*

Although the Bible has so often been used to reinforce women's "inferiority", women (and men) in the study groups also saw the Bible as the basis for belief in a new identity, an identity in Christ which transcends all social and cultural stereotypes and limitations. In the words of one group,

> We are convinced that a right proclamation of the gospel will lead to still increasing freedom and equality for women. *(Norway)*

The experience reported by one group illustrates the profound difference which can occur through reading the Bible from a new perspective:

> We pointed out the Galatians 3:28 passage along with Galatians 5:1 and many stories where women were treated as human beings by Paul and Jesus. A sixty-year old widow, hearing all these things, breathed a sign of great relief. "Why, that means that I am just as good as anyone." *(USA)*

"It is amazing", concluded a group from Lebanon, "how men cling to the ancient law and its concept of women. They forget that in Christ we are a new creation."

Human Wholeness

SUCH A LONG PROCESS TO BECOME THE IMAGE OF GOD

He said to her:
"You are precious in my eyes and glorious, because I love you"

and she became wife
and the mother of his sons

she became witch
and playmate
and the pale, shrouded virgin
of his dreams.
And she said to him:
"You are precious in my eyes and glorious, because I love you"

and he became lord
and master of her life

he became her husband
her horizon
her identity, her name.

And a world of love disappeared in a pond of Eden where each of them–entranced–stared lovingly at the image they had created.
God heard, saw, suffered, and said:
"You are precious in my eyes and glorious, because I love you."

Anna Marie Aagaard

Isaiah 43:4, New American Bible translation

INTRODUCTION

The consultation on "Towards a Theology of Human Wholeness" took place from 1 to 6 September 1980 at the Niederaltaich Benedictine Abbey in the beautiful Bavarian countryside near the Danube. The Abbey and its Ecumenical Centre were ideal hosts for the meeting since the community has a long commitment to Christian unity. As a sign of that commitment, part of the community lives by the Eastern rite while the other part continues in the tradition of St. Benedict. In addition, the monastery has recently received as a neighbour a community of Ursuline sisters who share in its spiritual and educational work.

The 18 participants from 15 countries included three Orthodox, seven Protestants and eight Roman Catholics–an indication of how important Catholics were to the entire Community Study process. Thirteen participants came from the North Atlantic and Mediterranean regions while five were from developing countries.

The following report is divided into two distinct sections. Section I –written by Constance Parvey, director of the Community Study programme–outlines the issues at stake in this consultation and describes the methodology used to address them. Section II is the actual consultation report written by the participants.

⋆ Major input for the consultation came from four papers presented at Niederaltaich. Three of these are printed in the July 1982 issue of *Mid-Stream: An Ecumenical Journal*: "*Imago Dei*" by Anna Marie Aagaard, "*The Imago Dei*: Two Historical Contexts" by Kari Elisabeth Bprresen, and "Towards a Theology of Human Wholeness in African Tradition" by Beatrice Luyombya. The fourth contribution–"Relationships Between Women and Men: Early Bangkok Period" by Maen Pongudom–can be obtained by writing to the Faith and Order Secretariat in Geneva.

I. THEOLOGICAL ANTHROPOLOGY: EXPLORING THE ISSUES

1. Addressing the theological problematic

A. Present experience

Women today have a growing awareness of the dissonance between past teachings of scripture and tradition regarding their nature and role and their own experience of themselves and their possibilities.

Women recognize:
1) that they are neither inferior nor superior to men;
2) that they are human persons and not to be defined primarily in terms of biological roles;
3) that they have capacities which constantly contradict the myths and stereotypes to which they have been so long subject.

Role expectations today are all too often based on unfounded assumptions regarding the superiority of male intelligence and strength and the narrowness or "otherness" or female abilities and vision. Emerging data from the biological and social sciences adds increasing support to many women's longstanding assumptions that most sex role differentiations are culture-relative and that psychological leanings are largely conditioned by societal and cultural conditioning.

Women's emerging sense of new personhood has created the need to explore afresh Christian teachings about women and to challenge the disparity between what women have been taught about "being woman" and what women experience their lives to be.

B. Theological inheritance

For growing numbers of Christian women today it is sobering to recognize the long centuries of masculine-shaped experience that allowed discrimination and subordination to flourish in spite of the liberating revelation of the Gospel of Jesus, the Christ.

It seems at first a simple matter to understand the central scriptural affirmations of the equality of all human persons before God. Not only the early church, but Christians down the centuries have asserted the value of each individual and the essential equality of persons as persons within the community of God's people. But at the same time that Christian theologians have affirmed the equality of each person, many have also taught an essential inequality between men and women. This theme in the history of Christian thought has placed men and women in a relationship of domination and subordination, and roles within church, family and society have been androcentric, hierarchical and gender-specific.

At the centre of this Christian teaching which has perpetutated the inequality of men and women is the doctrine of creation which on the one hand has affirmed the dignity of all human persons, but on the other has denied to women a full share in human nature. In the theological tradition of the "order of creation", it has been largely taken for granted that women are secondary to men–derivative, partial, "the other" in their identity as human persons (e.g., conventional interpretations and uses of Genesis 2).

The strongest rationale, however, for the subordination of women to men may be the failure of Christian theology to attribute to women the fullness of "the image of God". The Hebrew and Christian God is a transcendent God, neither male nor female. However, cultural and social realities which have given priority to men have also imaged the transcendent in primarily masculine terms. Whatever the efforts, then, to find in persons *qua* persons the image of God, the tendency has been to find in male persons the fullness of the image of God and in female persons the derivative, or reflected, image. The theological tradition has been androcentric and as a consequence the paradigm for the *Imago Dei* has been male personhood.

An additional consequence is that, rather than ascribing the fullness of personhood to women and to men, tradition has tended to place the male and female in dualistic opposition. Male persons have symbolized mind as opposed to body, strength as opposed to weakness, activity as opposed to passivity, autonomy as opposed to dependence. Tendencies in theology toward dualism (neo-Platonist) have developed these so-called "natural hierarchies" into a body-soul dichotomy.

The problematic before us is informed by contemporary life situations and is deeply rooted in Christian tradition. It confronts us with the challenging question: Can our present experience and traditional Christian affirmations meet? Is there an internal Christian anthropology that can make the leap between an androcentric cultural inheritance and contemporary equality movements?

2. Re-searching scripture and tradition for imagery of human wholeness

There are several points of entry into traditional Christian theology that offer new ways of understanding and living for both women and men and that call us to the task of re-presenting traditional theological affirmations

A. In the Bible

Central among these is an exploration of the fuller meaning of the "image of God". In Genesis 1, female and male together are created by God in God's image. Women and men are representative of a collective humanity and are co-equally models for the human. A re-presenting of this affirmation of human wholeness and mutuality is foundational for a renewed biblical and theological understanding of the fullness of human personhood for women and men.

B. In tradition

A thorough exploration of the *Imago Dei* is at the centre of this consultation. Its inter-relatedness with other theological issues also needs to be more fully investigated.

1) In Christology new enquiry is needed towards understanding the relationship of the historical Jesus, Jesus of Nazareth, to the risen Christ of faith. The maleness of the historical Jesus is a matter of past record, but does this mean that the resurrected Christ in the redeemed order of creation is identified with the male principle? Is the risen Christ, in whom the fullness of God was pleased to dwell, not a sign of the redemption of humanity, male and female, and an inclusive representative of new humanity for both women and men?
2) In Trinitarian theology the struggle throughout the centuries to deny subordinationism in God needs to be seriously explored for its promising anthropological implications for the corporate and relational life of women and men. Can contemporary theological reflection renew theological symbols so that they can give expression to contemporary understandings of God and human anthropology?
3) In the concept of the body of Christ in St Paul a rich metaphor of human partnership and social organization is suggested. Previous barriers of sex, religion, and economics are overcome (Galatians 3:27–28). Additionally, in this metaphor the variety of gifts is not

presented hierarchically, but in terms of integration and interdependence – body, mind, spirit. What are the links between the corporate teachings of being baptized into Christ and growing into the "image of God" as Christ is revealed in the New Creation (e.g., Ephesians 1:18–23, Colossians 1:15–29, Philippians 3:7–11)?

3. Examining the role of typologies in theological self-understanding

A. Mary

Mary, as symbol, has influenced the image and role of women. How has this served to reinforce women's circumscribed status, placing upon women full responsibility for nurturing and maintaining relationships in what is now the privatized sphere of home, family and children? Is there not an alternative image in the person of Mary: Mary as the public figure, the prophetess of the Magnificat, the one who lifts up a vision of renewal, who promises redemption from structures of oppression, who advocates and represents the liberated humanity of the church as New Creation? What is the significance of this Mary tradition for thinking about the fullness of personhood for women and about renewed relationships, public and private, between women and men?

B. Male and female typologies

What are the implications of traditional typologies for role expectations in church and society: e.g., Mary as the New Eve and Christ as the New Adam in early Christian thought; Mary as the model for women and Jesus as the model for men in popular piety; the representative Christ as the centre of the liturgy for the clergy and Mary as representative person for the laity in liturgical piety; or Christ as the bridegroom and the church as the bride in ecclesiology?

4. Towards a theology of human wholeness : methodology

Women and men, committed to the truth of the Gospel and seeking to understand what it means to be created as female and male in the image of God, must recognize that together we are called to live out this vision which God intends. The promise of new humanity in Christ calls us to be theologically responsible to our experience past and present, and invites us to anticipate, in our theological reflection and practice, the fulfilment of our human wholeness in God's New Creation.

As we move towards the vision of human wholeness and mutuality that God has intended for women and men, in addition to the research of scripture and tradition and new reflection on typologies, we must find our contemporary partners, such as :

a) Liberation theologies that also reflect on the present struggle in life situations in the light of scripture and tradition and with reference to the eschatological hope. Theologies of liberation need to be expanded to include the human liberation of all persons.

b) Insights obtainable from modern human experience and the sciences: equality and human rights movements, the technological revolution and the sexual revolution, insights from the human sciences and biology, and changing socio-economic structures. All of these challenge us to re-evaluate earlier anthropologies of sexuality, sex roles and partnership.

c) Insights from Christian experience in non-western cultures.

In the beginning God created humankind; male and female, God created them. God's will for us is that we be "one"–a community–in Christ Jesus. The vision of human wholeness for women and men towards which we move emerges out of this traditional affirmation of God's intention for humanity, and seeks, in partnership with present experience, its fulfilment in the New Creation revealed in Jesus, the Christ.

The purpose of the Niederaltaich consultation is to start an exploration of the resources available to help bridge the gap between an androcentric interpretation of this central theological affirmation and an inclusive anthropology of human wholeness (women and men, male and female) with insights from many cultures, human situations and churches. Though this is the first consultation of its kind to be held within the context of the World Council of Churches, the issues it raises were already raised at the first meeting of the WCC in Amsterdam, 1948, in a debate initiated by women in response to comments made by Karl Barth on Genesis 2. This consultation follows in the tradition of that earlier initiative.

The consultation methodology has three aspects:

First, it is based on two sources for theological reflection: contemporary human experience and the theological tradition. The starting point is reflection on contemporary experience with particular focus on the experience of women. This does not imply a goal of gyne-centric, as opposed to andro-centric, anthropology; but it does give recognition to the fact that the theological tradition has been dominated by the experience of men, and consequently that the experience of women needs to become a counter-focus of initiative in order to create a wider framework for the theological reflection that is authentic for both women and men. We need to allow, in dialogue and community, for the common and distinctive contributions of each.

Second, the methodology is based on a principle of correlation between experience, past and present, as our human contribution, and Divine intervention as God, the Holy Trinity, Maker of all things, guides the church in its praxis and teaching toward the unity and the renewal of human community.

Third, the consultation begins with the state of brokenness, with expressions of actual human conditions. Based on this acknowledged reality of brokenness, it then becomes possible to explore the resources for the transformation of the substance of our brokenness (evil) into that which is good. Thus the pursuit of theological wholeness in anthropology is also a pursuit of healing — of bodily transformation and transcendence.

Constance F. Parvey

II. THE CONSULTATION SPEAKS

1. The state of brokenness and the struggle for transformation

Confining patterns of dominance in our societies result in much suffering and oppression. Political, social, cultural, economic and religious patterns of domination often lead to dependence and to lack of freedom and self-determination, stultifying the creativity and growth of individuals and communities.

We find that experiences of subjection and oppression are universal, but they occur in different forms. It is different in third world and first world countries; it is also experienced differently by women. Poverty, dependence and oppression are experienced in third world countries, but debilitating forms of oppression are also found in the economically-powerful nations of the first world.

Church institutions, too, are part of this pattern in that we find inequality and injustice apparent in many aspects of our religious life, although in different ways in the different churches.

This report speaks about the *Imago Dei,* affirming that every human being is created in the image and likeness of God. However, it starts with descriptions of oppression and dominance because we are convinced that such social evils hinder the full realization of human potential. God has made us *Imago Dei*, but that dimension of God in us remains veiled when many in our world are oppressed and many others are oppressors. We also affirm that biblical thinking about *Imago Dei* is a powerful appeal for human growth and social transformation. Once each of us can realize that our neighbour, too, is made in God's image, then we are compelled to treat each other with mutual respect.

The statements that follow are written by individual participants. They are personal statements and reflect how the state of brokenness is experienced–particularly the subordination of women–in various countries and communions. These statements are offered with the conviction that assessments of our state of brokenness are themselves steps toward wholeness.*

A. Statements from participants in various countries

The following statements, offered by participants during the Niederaltaich consultation, should be seen as informed, personal reflections and not as fully-developed analyses.

1. Latin America

Patterns of dominance and oppression are so wide-spread in contemporary Latin America that one is hesitant even to speak of the *Imago Dei* in this context. Corrupted, self-interested political systems have, through long years of economic exploitation and class division, denied people the possibility for basic human self-validation.

Women have been the most direct victims of injustices. The lack of a real sense of identity begins at birth when the fact of being born female already implies rejection and inferiority. A female is considered as an object that can be fondled–first by her parents and then, as a young wife, by her husband. As an adult woman she often sees no other meaning for her life than hard work. She frequently lacks real affection and may thus live without hope. The daily experience of isolated suffering hardens her personality and is accepted by her as fate. Everything, being the will of God, is going to remain as it is.

* The term "wholeness", as used in this report, is not intended to mean the opposite of physical or psychological disability. The loss of a limb or psychological depression does not necessarily impair the wholeness of a person. When we use the term "wholeness", we have in mind St Paul's description of community as the integrated members of the one body of Christ.

This attitude is especially prevalent in the lower classes where the oppression of the socio-economic structures is felt most intensely.

The oppression of women is found as well in the upper class, where it takes the form of prejudices which restrict personal growth. Myths about women's identity and role have an especially powerful effect in the upper class. Mass media reinforce these myths and, thus, manipulate the lives of these women.

The presence of the churches, both Catholic and Protestant, has done little to alleviate the oppression of women. In many places, the "good news" about human freedom, as recorded in Luke 4, has not been announced. The Gospel as the *dynamus* for salvation (Romans 1:16), for the creation of a "new being", has not been presented in such a way that it can affect positively the life of all, women and men.

Since the Gospel has generally been presented only in terms of "good and evil", people in Latin America are often trapped in a moralistic stage that does not permit them to become whole persons. The biblical concern for justice and injustice has often been left out of the church's preaching and teaching. Women have not been able to see who they are, or what their condition really is. This means they are not yet ready to participate in social change.

In addition, the very structures of the church are another major obstacle to the full realization of the *Imago Dei* in women. These structures, in which women are forced to play subordinate roles, hinder women from exercising their individual gifts–gifts which are given by the Spirit, gifts which might be used to build up the body of Christ. What is needed is a return to the message of the scriptures-that the church is a living body made up of participating members, women and men, equally created and affirmed in God's image.

2. Thailand

Four big enemies challenge the long process of becoming *Imago Dei* today in Thailand.

First, 100,000 refugees from our neighbouring countries–Vietnam, Laos and Kampuchea–are crying for mercy and justice. They are dehumanized by demonic, destructive power. They are not only physically naked, shelterless and hungry, but also spiritually tortured. Their tears are not only tears, but also the blood of Abel!

Second, the gap between the "haves" and "have-nots" becomes wider and wider due to the uncontrolled greed of the oligarchy and the rich few. Middle-men use their right hands to grasp the necks of the producers while their left hands twist the empty stomachs of the consumers. Poor beggar Lazarus and the greedy rich!

Third, freedom of creativity is suppressed by our rulers. Books that could provide intellectual stimulation and consciousness-raising are thrown away like garbage. The "tree of wisdom" is in the process of *bonsai*. The rulers want to tame their people like they tame their dogs at home, but at least they teach their dogs to be clever!

Finally, the desire to escape from poverty (coupled with ignorance) has led thousands of girls from the country to be massage-parlour prostitutes. Sexual affairs become a business and a profession. The so-called "modernization" of Thailand has made Bangkok a place of "international bed-affairs". When you look through the glass walls of the massage parlours, you do not see the beautiful *Imago Dei*, but dehumanized creatures with numbers and prices. The *Imago Dei* is without numbers, and it is priceless!

3. New Zealand

Oppression is not only found in those countries known as the third world. Patterns of dominance, oppression and injustice are found also among the affluent; peace and security do not necessarily encourage individuals and communities to grow into the *Imago Dei*.

New Zealand is a small country on the distant edge of the world. It is a nation of only three million people, in a rich and fertile land, without refugees, great extremes of wealth and poverty, beggars, or political prisoners. Those who live there often call it "God's own". Yet, in the midst of freedom and plenty, people still struggle in the process of becoming *Imago Dei*.

We are afraid of losing our comfortable way of life, fearful of becoming poor and vulnerable. Thus, we are oppressed by economic and political self-interest, measuring our success and happiness in terms of gross national product.

We are also dominated, politically and economically, by foreign powers and international corporations. Needing trade, oil, and military defense, we sell our forests, pollute our rivers, and destroy our wildlife (some of which has already become extinct). We allow secret military bases to be installed on our land and nuclear submarines to be sheltered in our harbours.

And we, too, oppress. The Maori people–the original inhabitants of "New Zealand", now a dispossessed ethnic minority–are forced to struggle against the loss of their land, identity and language. Similar discrimination is directed toward Polynesian immigrants who find it difficult to maintain identity and dignity in an alien culture. Then there are the thousands of Asian refugees, our neighbours, who struggle just to keep alive while we do nothing.

Women, too, struggle in this patriarchal society–for the right to control their own bodies and lives.

We have been fearful of opening ourselves to the suffering of others, fearful of finding the wounded Christ in the face of our neighbour. Even in our first world culture, we struggle with various forms of oppression. Here, too, it is a slow and difficult process to become what we are called to be–the image of God.

B. The situation in various communions: statements from participants

1. The Church of Greece

In order to present the condition of women in modern Greece, it is necessary to bear in mind the historical fact that four centuries of Ottoman rule created a way of life in which women came to have a far from enviable situation. Nevertheless, rapid changes in the country during 150 years of independence, and especially since the Second World War, have led to a significant improvement in their status. Women have access to university studies, including theology, and women teach on theological faculties. Their presence is felt in the fields of art, politics, science and teaching. There has been a renewal of the diaconate of women through the foundation of a Higher School for Deaconesses and Social Assistants. There is also a strong revival of the monastic life, as young women–some of them highly educated and professionally trained–are entering it and making an impact on church life. Furthermore, a number of women's movements (e.g., the Y.W.C.A. and various student unions, associations of university-trained women, etc.) are working on vital issues, especially those concerning women.

Community life is experienced by men and women working together either within organized movements whose objectives are, at one and the same time, educational, social and cultural, or within groups set up on their own initiative. The aim of the latter is to consider present-day problems in the light of the Orthodox tradition by means of studies, conferences, publications, and so on.

In the field of parish life, women participate actively through work with the poor, the sick, the aged and needy families. They prepare the bread for the eucharist and the boiled wheat for the commemoration of the dead. They lead their children to liturgy from their infancy. This is true as well in the big urban centres, where secularization is proceeding at an increasing pace.

In Greece there is little demarcation between church and society. Thus a woman who has the opportunity to develop, either inside or outside the parish, feels fulfilment in her role. She does not therefore look upon ordination to the priesthood as a goal–she can be ordained to other roles. In the Orthodox understanding, the church is not coincidental with the clergy. The church is the people of God–clergy and laity together. For this reason women take little heed of traditional attitudes towards them. They pay little attention to the ancient Old Testament influence of a sexually discriminatory nature, or the prayers read to them at childbirth. They overlook the fact that infant girls, unlike baby boys, are not allowed to the altar.

There is no doubt that with proper instruction women could become fully conscious of their responsibilities as church members and be able to assume them. What now seems to be urgent for the women in Greece is:

a) Continued in-depth study by theologians, men and women, on Orthodox anthropology, which could contribute to research on theological anthropology on the ecumenical level.
b) The commitment of the living elements in the church, both by clergy and laity, to a common search for the meaning of the "royal priesthood" (I Peter 2:9) and the forms it can take for women and men in the concrete reality of the present.

2. The Orthodox Church in France

Within a common doctrinal framework the status of women in the different Orthodox churches varies according to historical and sociocultural factors. The Orthodox archbishopric in France, under the jurisdiction of the Ecumenical Patriarchate, grew from the "Russian Emigration", but is today fully integrated into French society. It has the benefit of a liberal internal regulation (adopted by the Russian Church in 1917, on the eve of the Revolution) that is particularly concerned to associate lay persons with church responsibilities. Since women are also *laikos*, they are full members of the people of God; they are in no way excluded from these responsibilities. Women serve, for example, as elected members of various parish councils, and can even co-preside with the priest in charge of the community. In this way, women become part of the diocesan assembly called to elect the bishops.

Within the parish, women assume numerous responsibilities–in the education of children, in the preparation of the parish newsletter, in the direction of the parish choir (a most important task in the framework of Orthodox liturgy), in diaconia. They do not, however, have the right to preach, although this right is recognized for laymen through delegation by the bishop. For some years, women have had access to higher theological education, both as students and as professors. But, until now, no woman has ever been entrusted with teaching systematic theology. Women professors are relegated to teaching positions of a "secondary" nature, e.g., languages and, in some cases, philosophy. Similarly, in the parishes, women are expected to take charge, for the most part, of material tasks or tasks of execution rather than responsibilities which imply theological reflection and intellectual inventiveness.

Still, an evolution of basic attitudes can be perceived. For example, a group of lay persons (among whom women are the large majority) recently published an innovative catechism without the church hierarchy having intervened directly in the process of its production. The idea of "conciliarity" which is characteristic of Orthodox ecclesiology works in favour of such transformations–although sometimes it works too slowly for our liking. Conciliarity demands a genuine consensus that grows out of the talents and input of many church members, both women and men.

It must be noted–whether one deplores or applauds it–that, at the present time, there exists no aggressive feminism within the Orthodox communities in France. There are, however, small dynamic groups, made up of men and women, which challenge the church in a variety of ways. Among their major concerns are the following:

a) the persistence of the idea of women's ritual impurity, especially as this is expressed in interdicts;
b) the exclusion of women from all liturgical functions–such as serving as a reader or acolyte–which depend on ordination or, simply, on a benediction;*

* In actual practice, women often do exercise these functions, though they are excluded from them in theory.

c) the refusal to discuss, on a serious theological basis, the question of the ordination of women to the ministerial priesthood;
d) the refusal to restore the diaconate of women, a diaconate which existed in the ancient church.

3. The Roman Catholic Church in Italy

The situation of women in the Catholic Church in Italy is a contradication, due in part to the separation which still exists between clergy and laity. On the one hand, doctrinal principles and the declarations of the hierarchy are clearly discriminatory against women; on the other hand, there is much pressure for greater participation of women on all levels of church life, and this has led to a few practical results in some dioceses and parishes. It is in the area of Christian education that these results are most apparent (though here, too, the involvement of women is not based on official church decisions). Charitable work is also entrusted to women. This type of work is not seen, however, as a first step towards the recognition of non-ordained ministries for women (e.g. reader and acolyte), although these same ministries are recognized for men. It must be underlined here that, though women suffer greater discrimination, their situation is fundamentally the same as that of the entire laity; both lay men and women are generally used only for practical tasks.

The fact of engaging women for practical tasks, and especially for the Christian education of children, raises two problems:

a) In response to women's demands for equal participation, the church hierarchy can answer that women are already sufficiently engaged in the life of the church. This then becomes an excuse for preventing full participation by women in such areas as liturgy, decision-making and the elaboration of doctrine.
b) The involvement of women gives men an alibi for not sharing in the responsibility of religious education. Such sharing is essential if we are to avoid the continuation of male-female stereotypes and the continued separation of sexual roles.

In Italy, new communities, based on sharing and equality, are being formed. Some try to stay within the church, others are splitting from it. It is our conviction that the church urgently needs to learn from these new attempts at integrated Christian community life at parish levels.

4. The Churches in Scandinavia

Equality of the sexes exists in theory and also, to a large extent, in practice within Scandinavian society; but there is a marked disparity in Norway, Denmark and Sweden between social reality and theological anthropology. A striking example is that the 1978 Norwegian law concerning the equality of sexes makes an exception for the church communities and in Sweden a minority of Lutheran pastors, led by one bishop, is strongly opposing the ordination of women.

The Roman Catholic Church is a minority in the nordic countries. (In Norway, for example, there are only approximately 13,000 members). Paradoxically, this church, of which the doctrinal and juridical body is the most androcentric, shows the least tension between the clerical hierarchy and the laity in the question which concerns us here. The Scandinavian Bishops Conference maintains a pastoral attitude well adapted to Scandinavian social realities. An example is the letter addressed by the bishops to the faithful regarding the encyclical *Humanae Vitae* (1968), a letter that stressed the judgment of personal conscience. In turn, Scandinavian Catholic bishops try to inform the centralized bodies in Rome of the socio-cultural situation in which their faithful live, often with a view to a necessary *aggiornamento* on the doctrinal and pastoral levels.

5. The Kongo Society of Zaire

The traditional Kongo society tends to subordinate women to men. Several facets of traditional Kongolese society–polygamy, the dowry, the demand for virginity on the wedding day, the double standard of sexual morality–reveal this subordinate position. It must be stressed, however, that while in the total cultural context woman is placed on the level of a child, within the clan and the conjugal home, she is not inferior to a man. To a great extent, the clan revolves around her. Within the clan, no decision can be made without her participation and agreement. Within the conjugal home, there is a division of work which democratizes human relationships. Extra-marital relations (tolerated only during the woman's pregnancy and the period of breast-feeding) which are not consented to by the woman, could lead to severe sanctions on her husband. The woman could even demand a divorce.

Within the clan and the conjugal home, the man and the woman each retains his or her own role, duties and name. This allows for a strong sense of personal identity. Neither man nor woman is tied to the other, but only to the clan. Furthermore, traditional Kongo culture does not impose any sexist language. Each is a *Muntu* (person), all possess the same vital strength which helps them to become *Nganga* (priest, medium, healer) and *Knulu* (ancestor) according to their qualities and virtues.

Unfortunately, the patriarchal character of the colonial administration and of the western missionary churches has altered the positive elements of the traditional relationship between women and men. It is true that the dowry, polygamy and division of work have also been modified, but their traditional symbolism has given way, not to equality, but to the commercialization of the woman. The new division of work, for example, is not proving to be an instrument for the democratization of relationships, but rather a structure for the control and subordination of women.

At present, within the church, there are women who serve as Sunday School leaders and consecrated parish pastors, founders and spiritual leaders of ecclesial communities. But, for the most part, the ecclesiastical structures are still too much influenced by the traditional tendencies of male domination and western, patriarchal biblical teaching.

Matriarchy has been characteristic, at least within the clan, of Kongo society and of several other African cultures. We suggest that this pattern of matriarchal society (which is often reflected in the community life of the African independent churches), along with the rich store of African myths and creation stories, offer new, potentially fruitful areas of research as we look for revitalized images of God and new forms of human community.

C. Struggle for transformation

As Christians we see the power that heals, supports and redeems, not the power that oppresses and destroys. We believe in the potentially transforming power of the Christian vision of the *Imago Dei*. This power must not be used for domination and oppression but for service and the growth of freedom. Yet for this we must struggle. Although the situation of women varies widely in different cultural contexts, women often have no power to name and determine themselves, to live a life of self-respect and dignity. As these personal testimonies show, the traditional language of the church, the various forms of liturgy and theology (which have been developed by men), and the authority structures of church institutions have given some, but limited, room to women. Women remain a silent majority of the churches. In many instances, the churches speak on behalf of women, but do not yet listen to women or allow women to speak authoritatively for themselves.

An aspect of the struggle for transformation can be seen in the phenomenon of new types of communities parallel to or outside of the churches which are emerging in the West, primarily among young adults. These small groups, women and men, attempt to live together without discrimination, sharing goods and responsibilities. A certain spontaneity exists within these groups; they are open and, in general, most hospitable. In some cases, members of the group work at joint projects; in other instances, each member pursues his or her own professional activity. It is important to emphasize that these groups are, at least in part, an attempt to overcome the stereotyped structures of the church and of traditional attitudes towards relationships and family patterns.

Integral to the process of transformation is the need to analyze what blocks the process toward human wholeness, theologically, and then suggest what could move us forward. What follows is such an initial attempt.

2. The image of God

A. Mental structures re-considered

Mental structures and patterns of thought prevalent in society and in the churches often determine the identity of women on the basis of that of men. These prior mental structures are a particular feature of the western churches (and of those that issued from the West). In these churches, the exegesis of the biblical texts relating to man and woman has created a discriminatory theological anthropology which has influenced doctrinal considerations and been transmitted in the teaching of the church. In Orthodox churches, the basic position is more nuanced, and the understanding of women is due more to ecclesiastical traditions than to doctrinal teaching.

It is absolutely essential, therefore, if the biblical message is to maintain its credibility, that the relevant scriptural texts be re-examined. Such a re-analysis should be done by women and men together at all levels of church life–from academic research to local biblical study. This must be done with the guidance of the Holy

Spirit and with the conviction that God's revelation in Christ is an ongoing and dynamic process in the church. Such re-analysis must take into account the significantly altered world-wide context which, on the one hand, is pluri-cultural and yet, on the other, is united in its dependence on modern technological, social and economic systems.

We suggest that some of these "mental structures" be re-examined to take into account the following realizations:

1) That mutuality between women and men is often described by the term "complementarity". This is a potentially dangerous term because of the connotation it carries that the woman is the "complement" (or helpmate, or appendage) of man. It is a basic necessity that each becomes a "self" in order to grow in partnership and service to each other.

2) That theological anthropology founded on such a re-examination often encounters resistance from the "institutional church", an organization that is inherently of a stabilizing, conservative nature. Wholeness in anthropology must, therefore, be worked out in a necessary "dialectical" relation between the institutions as such and the prophetic dynamism in the *Imago Dei*.

3) That the development of new anthropological models must be based on a dialogue between the churches that have long-standing traditions and the younger churches seeking their own identities, and between traditional theological positions and theologies from the women's movement and third world movements.

4) That all re-examination must be done in continuity with the tradition. It must move, however, beyond traditional divisions to draw upon the resources of the whole and undivided church. In this way, the search for an anthropology of human wholeness may undergird the ecumenical steps for a visible unity of all churches within the context of renewed community.

B. Describing God through integrated models

We are aware of the fact that the exclusively male images of God in the mostly western Christian tradition have supported the affirmation of male, white, western superiority and have led to a sense of inferiority of women, of the poor, and of people from non-western cultures. There is, therefore, an urgent need–as persons and as community–to reach for descriptions of God that reflect the contemporary desire for wholeness. We need ways of describing and experiencing God that touch the mystery, the creative potential, the relational longings of our spiritual lives.

In searching the tradition, some possibilities begin to emerge. These are not exhaustive, but we do hope that they are suggestive of the kinds of identity with God that we seek.

1) *God as Creator* is a way of relating to God that may inspire our human creativity; it is a description that motivates us to become co-operators, partners, co-creators with God. This is also a cosmic model for understanding God's activity. It reminds us that God's creative presence extends to all creation–nature, earth, sky–and thus it implies that the responsibility God gave us of stewardship over creation is not to be perverted into forms of dominance and objectification. Such stewardship implies the task of integrating cosmic and community life.
2) *God, as the Holy Trinity*, is relational. This is, of course, an ancient teaching but, when seen in light of the modern search for new community, it takes on renewed importance. God is perceived as a "centre of relations", as the interaction of Father, Son and Holy Spirit which makes up the oneness of the living God. Each human person is also a centre of relations. It is in the interaction with others that we come to know God and ourselves. It is, thus, the relational God of the Trinity who reveals our relational nature and calls us to build up an integrated society.
3) Genesis 1:27 (*So God created humankind in God's image*; in God's image, male and female, God created them) implies that we may think of God in androgynous terms. Since God created the human being as male and female in the divine image, we may certainly suggest that God,too, has both male and female aspects. To be both male and female is linked with what it means to be in God's image and, conversely, our maleness and femaleness can point us towards God. This image calls us to recognize the fundamental equality or women and men as *Imago Dei*, but it also challenges us to acknowledge and develop the male and female aspects within each person. This twofold nature of each individual is also a reflection of the divine.
4) *Christ as the Eikon*, the image of God, may be the best model for us as a Christian community in our struggle to become a holistic and prophetic community. Historically, Jesus lives as a "model-breaker" in continuity with the prophetic tradition. Through him we continue to experience God's option for the oppressed and

God's rejection of all powers of dominance. "Call no man your father on earth.... He who is greatest among you shall be your servant; whoever exalts himself will be humbled and whoever humbles himself will be exalted" (Matthew 23:9-12). This emptying out of power into service to others implies that the male symbol for God is here undergoing its own *kenosis*. As God, through Christ, is emptied out in suffering service, so the Divine Logos is emptied of power in becoming the Christ; and as Christ is no longer identified as male, it is through the people of God that the ongoing messianic presence in the world is represented. This transfer of messianic identity to the community implies our shared suffering in the struggle for liberation; our prophetic-messianic calling as women and men makes us co-sufferers with Christ in God's continuing work to manifest renewed community.

Christ, then, is our central image of the *Imago Dei* through whom we can each become a new being "having put on the new nature, which is being renewed in knowledge after the image of its creator" (Colossians 3:10). We are called to imitate Christ by "forgetting everything except Jesus Christ and especially his death on the cross" (I Corinthians 2:2).

C. Some pastoral consequences of partial description

Our pastoral experience also shows, however, that a partial or warped understanding of Jesus the Christ-as-model can lead to some negative consequences:

1) *Looking at the cross can lead to a wrongly understood commitment.* Many Christians, for example, feel obliged to commit themselves so totally for others that they destroy themselves. Such commitment, far from being altruistic, is often a futile way of hiding the emptiness of their hearts and of finding recognition in the greatness of their dedication.

   Scripture tells us over and over again that the love of one's neighbour has its limits in the love of oneself. Only in so far as you "suffer yourself" are you free to be able to "suffer others". Our ability of "suffering ourselves" is based on the fact that God loves us, that God has suffered for us. God has said "yes" to ourselves as women and men, even though we are still so far from our goal. The encounter with God in Jesus the Christ enables us to encounter others; and by experiencing the other person as a "you", we find our "I".

2) *Looking at the cross can lead to a wrongly understood rigidity.* Many Christians feel obliged to respond to Christ's sacrifice for us with such a strict asceticism that they become "hard" to themselves and others. Such asceticism, far from being God's will, may simply be a way of becoming insensitive.

   Jesus demonstrates, however, that salvation begins by opening one's eyes and ears. By opening our senses, God makes us more sensitive and at the same time more vulnerable. It is a sign of hope when, despite this vulnerability, we become neither isolated nor aggressive. Only through this awakened sensitivity can we remain receptive to the experiences of God's salvation.

   This sensitivity can and must be recognized in a variety of settings. It is essential for all forms of Christian community–for family life, for marriage, and also for Christian celibacy. Monasticism, for example, can represent this combination of sensitivity and vulnerability and can, thus, be a sign of hope for the church. It points towards an openness which is the precondition for experiencing the fullness of life through faith in God's caring love.

3) *Looking at the cross of Christ can lead to a wrongly understood refusal of creation.* Many Christians understand the message of Christ's death on the cross as a prophetic appeal to change the world in such a way that all threats and manipulation will end for all people. Such commitment to the "rule of God's word", however, may lead only to an attempt to suppress emotions and passions instead of changing them into love which is the fundamental motivation of prophecy.

   The early church also stressed that in Jesus Christ God's Word has been expressed in the "icon" of human beings. In human beings created in God's image, critical rationality and emotional sensitivity can be reconciled and human life can find its integrity in all its dimensions. The crucified one is rooted in the bosom of the earth, his arms of suffering outstretched in love to embrace the whole cosmos (cf. Matthew 12:40, Ephesians 3:18).

D. It's a long process to become Imago Dei

As Christians, we believe that every human being is created in the image and likeness of God. Even in the midst of our struggles against inequality and oppression, our belief in this is continually strengthened. To approach human beings as *Imago Dei* provides us with a vision of hope. It also provides us with a goal, since the realization of this image involves a long process of becoming and growth. The

Christian vision of the *Imago Dei* is an invitation, and powerful appeal, to work for what we are not yet, to grow towards, a fuller, more authentic personal and communal life in order to enable this divine image to become more transparent. We as individuals cannot become the *Imago Dei* without, at the same time, helping others to become truer to this image. Thus, this image offers a dynamic vision for transforming ourselves, for creating new dimensions of our identity as women and men within community.

For us the image of God is most fully experienced in Christ: "Christ is the visible likeness of the invisible God" (Colossians 1:15). The image of Christ has different faces; at the same time it is human and divine, female and male, a face of suffering, poverty and sacrifice, but also a face of love and hope, of grace, joy, power and glory. We do not, finally, have the power to transform ourselves, but through Jesus the Christ we see the hand of God that shapes us into becoming what we are not yet. God shapes us through what we undergo and suffer as well as through what we build up and create. In all our moments, the power of God is at work in transforming us.

It is a long process to become the image of God. It is a process that involves suffering, crucifixion and death, as well as the transforming power of God's resurrection and redemption. Christ, present in each of us, helps us to grow together to full stature. This growth occurs as we participate in that which builds new community, and it is only through such growth that new community–new creation–will finally be fashioned.

As our experience comes to bear on the re-describing and re-telling of the Christ event, a process of re-discovery of the *Imago Dei* is set in motion. Coming into community from our many cultures and communions we bring to each other a rich treasury of perspectives and interpretations that enlarge our vision of *Imago Dei* and encourage us to continue our pursuit for human wholeness precisely at those points where we are the most broken. With this in mind, we turn our attention to the "shadow side of woman".

3. Towards a true image: redemption of the shadow side of God

A. The shadow side of woman

In the search for a true community of women and men, we have learned that we must begin first with the psychological and biological realities of our brokenness.

Psychologically speaking, over-emphasized patriarchal tendencies have thrown a shadow on the life-giving biological productivity of women by projecting an "unclean spirit" or a "shadow side" on her and thus demeaning her natural creativity. This verdict has contributed to inner schism, to a loss of security and trust, and to unnecessary feelings of tension and isolation.

This conflict within a woman's own innermost nature has naturally affected the relationships between women and men. The suffering caused by disturbances of close and meaningful relationships, the growth of fears and narcissism, and the increase of psychosomatic illness and psychosis are, in part, the results of this rupture and repression.

Biologically speaking, we have learned from those who work in the healing professions that positive bodily experiences can be broken, and have been broken, by structural attitudes. For the purposes of this report, we offer only one example: menstruation and its supposed "uncleanness".

Biologically, to a modern medical doctor, menstruation means three things:

1) It is the external evidence that the woman is not pregnant.
2) It signals the new possibility (or risk) of becoming pregnant.
3) It is the external sign that a woman's hormones are working properly.

We have found, however, that in many cultures–in Africa, Asia, Europe, and North America–menstruation is, or has been, labelled as something "dirty", something that requires an act of purification. Daughters around the world, upon receiving their first period, have been told by their mothers that "this is an affliction (or punishment) that all women must live with". The menstruating woman is often thought to be "bad" or even "dangerous" in some contexts. In some cultures, she is not allowed to cook or to mix with other people. It is believed that grass will wither if she walks on it and that milk will sour if she touches it. Threatening and powerful things are thought to come from her body. In some cultures, for example, menstrual blood is considered to be attractive for evil spirits and, thus, women are often used as mediums.

These superstitions have frequently found their way into the church. It has been argued that women should not have access to "sacred space or 'rites'" partly because of their "uncleanness" during menstruation.

A closely related problem is that women's bodies are often regarded as "things"; women come to see their own bodies as objects that don't measure up to social expectations. Many women fear, for example, that their breasts are too small, or that their genitals are too large, for them to be accepted by men. What this means is that women are not allowed to determine their own physical ideal; it is determined by men and by male projections of the "ideal woman".

Men also suffer from this imposed ideal. If, for instance, a man's penis is not of a certain size, he is thought to be a poor lover. The effect of this is that in some cultures, diapers are not used on male infants for fear that they will prevent normal growth of the penis. The lives of both women and men are distorted psychologically and physically by caricatured models of the "ideal man"/"ideal woman".

B. The shadow side of culture: dualistic theology

"The shadow side of women", as a metaphor for uncleanness and separation, points to the need for new metaphors that go beyond the traditional dualisms of western thought which assign women to a lower rank: light/dark, body/soul, self/other, rational/intuitive, clean/unclean, male/female. Such dualistic thinking may have served a purpose in the development of western culture, but it now serves to hamper the growth toward a new community characterized by wholeness and partnership. Dualistic, hierarchical thinking did not, by itself, lead to the oppression of women; women have traditionally been relegated to a subordinate status even in many non-western cultures and religions. But dualistic thinking, a pattern of thought which identifies one group by its opposition to another, is characteristic of the western context within which women are now struggling for liberation.

Such thinking, at its worst, serves to "stratify" and "objectify" human beings and their environment. It is a way of perceiving that breaks reality into compartments–a time for play *or* a time for work, a time for intimacy *or* a time of uncleanness. It is a way of perceiving that inevitably leads to hierarchical systems–mind is placed *above* body, light *above* darkness, activity *above* passivity. It is a way of perceiving that causes people–particularly men–to view the world, and the persons in it, as "things" to be manipulated and controlled. One obvious example is the dualistic separation of "man" and "nature" that has led to an exploitation of natural resources–the use of power against nature rather than its development as God's creation.

Dualistic thinking has, of course, had devastating implications for women. As many scholars have pointed out, whenever such thinking has prevailed, women (being without political or economic power) are placed on the negative side of a hierarchy of values. They are "classed as passive, irrational, illogical, soft, introvert and pertaining to the dark principle" (Kurt Lüthi)–all of which are considered inferior to their "opposed", "masculine" values. Women have, thus, been seen as helpmates or "complements" or "appendages" (e.g., Adam's rib) of men, but seldom as beings that are, themselves, fully in the image of God.

Dualistic thinking has also meant that women have been regarded as objects, as "the other", who stand over against the dominant male perspective of western art, philosophy and science; and their bodies have often been seen as things either to be glorified or used for a particular purpose–usually procreation or pleasure. In sexual relations, as well as in public life, women are relegated to inferior, dependent roles.

We think it is important to realize that this dualistic thinking, with its stereotypes of what is female, is constantly being exported through advertising and entertainment to non-western cultures. Everyone is familiar with advertisements in which partially-clad women are used to draw attention to a product. And everyone has seen movies in which beautiful (passive, soft, illogical) women serve as the reward for male bravery or accomplishment, or as instruments for male betrayal. Such images, when mass produced in non-western settings, tend to reinforce a low status and distrustful attitude towards women in these cultures.

The contemporary church is both a cause and an effect of this dualistic thinking. (Church structures reflect that heritage of neo-Platonism and philosophical idealism even as they perpetuate these patterns of thought by according them ecclesiastical sanction.) Despite the undeniable fact that Jesus broke through the religious and political hierarchical structures of his day, and that he called his followers to deny traditional forms of hierarchy and separation, the later church proceeded to elevate soul above body, clergy above laity, strength above weakness, masculine above feminine. And in its encounter with other cultures, the church has often seen the world in dualistic terms. African religions or Hindu faith have been viewed as "alien", "dark" "primitive" and, consequently, to be avoided or denied. With this mental structure, the church has until now learned little from non-western cultures, even when these might provide rich resources for moving beyond dualistic patterns of thought. In fact, Christian teaching has tended to give theological sanction to subordination of women in Africa and Asia.

It is our opinion that Christian teaching must recover a vision of theology that is based not on dualistic, hierarchical separation, but on wholeness and integration. One place to start such a task is with an exploration of renewed images of God, of God's image in humanity, and God's hope for human community. Such images, of course, cannot be fabrications; authentic images grow out of scripture and tradition, and from their encounter with the lived, multicultural experience of the community of faith. We understand revelation as that which continues, in that each generation must comprehend anew its engagement with the living God. We believe that the time is now right–with the secular women's movements, the widespread threats of dehumanization, the challenging, intensifying interaction among cultures–for the birth of a renewed community, beyond dualism, reconciled through Christ in God.

C. The shadow side of God

"The shadow side of God" is a provisional metaphor in our search for renewed images and for a community based on wholeness. God reaches down into the depths of the "shadow side" of life and calls captive life into new energy and freedom. Out of the depths, God calls us to live in courage as spiritual correspondents and co-creators in the liberation, redemption and integration of the whole creation.

Christian life is lived out, not as a dualistic struggle, but as a dance of duality. In women, that dance is experienced concretely in bodily life. As the blood of menstruation is viewed by custom and law as unclean and alienating, so the same life blood is a sign of God's renewing creation of life–promise, expectation, eternity. As the menstrual cycle of a woman may, by custom and convention, bring separation and alienation, so the menstrual cycle is cosmically connected with the deepest revolutions of nature and the most fundamental continuity of human life. As the pregnant woman moans, groans and suffers in travail for the life of the child she does not yet see, so God calls into partnership all those who suffer in hope.

This unending dance of dualities is lived out, not as an otherworldly expectation, but as a concrete dialectic between faith and experience here and now. Scripture uses the allusion of the woman in childbirth as a metaphor for new creation, life and kinship with God (Romans 8:22). This aspect of a woman's bodily existence–so surrounded with culturally established taboos, uncleanness, exclusion and "thingification"–is the very aspect that is lifted up and chosen to announce and make known the way in which the suffering God works *with, in* and *through* bodily life for the Great Transformation. What was formerly considered the "shadow side of woman" is redescribed and transformed into a metaphor of hope and new creation for all who are in tribulation, distress, persecution and famine. Through this power of re-telling, we experience that God lives through us and with us in the struggle against all forms of oppression and dualism. Through God's living Word, we find the strength and wisdom to reconcile the extremes of old and new creation and, in the act of so doing, the living image of Christ becomes transparent.

Through the Holy Spirit, God calls the church to the depths of its true bodily and reconciling nature–communal, reconciling, ever renewing. The *Imago Christi* includes all people. In the suffering Jesus and risen Christ, we see God living out the longing for the full integration of each of us, woman and man, in our coming to fullness of life in *Imago Dei*.

As women and men we acknowledge that we are the same, yet different. As Christians, from our different communions, we find that we are in agreement to pursue a holistic, theological anthropology, but we are not yet in complete understanding as to what difference our biological differences make from a theological and typological perspective. What follows is an orthodox contribution, a theological affirmation that is both a basis for agreement and an occasion for continuing dialogue.

D. ORTHODOX AFFIRMATION: THE MYSTERY OF PERSONS AND ROLE OF TYPOLOGY

Founded in the Gospel, in the continuity of the living tradition of the church, Orthodox anthropology–according to its fundamental dynamics–is not androcentric but theocentric. What constitutes the human being *(anthropos)* in his or her true humanity is the image of God imprinted in all persons. This is not merely a part or function

(e. g., intelligence) of the human being. It is a "mystery", according to Gregory of Nyssa's expression, a mystery which we turn around when we speak of the driving force of the human person–man or woman–towards the Living God. Here we must stress the radically apophatic nature of Orthodox theology. This extends itself to what we could call an apophatic anthropology which insists on the mystery of persons and of the relationship between those persons.

Human persons, female and male, are created and recreated by baptism in Christ who is the image of the Father–the Unique Son. Human beings are made in the image of God and are drawn towards God's resemblance by that within them, the desire of Absolute Love, which is an opening towards the Transcendent. Gregory of Nyssa compares the human being–*anthropos*– to a mobile mirror which, if it turns towards God (and this is the meaning of the word conversion), becomes completely luminous and illuminates the world. From this perspective, it is important that a woman, Mary, according to ecclesial typology, represents the church which is humanity saved in hope. This means that as we, men and women, come face to face with the Living God, we are called to an attitude of openness and humble obedience of which the feminine is the symbol. We are saved with the help of that which in each one of us opens itself to mysterious wedlock with the Spirit.

There is no doubt, however, that neither the practice nor the official declarations of the historical Orthodox churches, nor of those who have spoken in their name, have always honoured this vision. Cultural conditioning and the natural hardness of hearts, have prevented its incarnation in an ethic of reciprocity and mutual respect, particularly with regard to man-woman relationships. We constantly need to convert ourselves to the celestial vision, and then to invent creative ways of incarnating that vision in our existence. To be conscious of this summons and this task seems essential for today's orthodoxy, in which, whatever our failings, the Magnificat of Mary never ceases to resound like a song of hope.

LIST OF PARTICIPANTS

Prof. Anna Marie AAGAARD, Denmark
Dr. Elisabeth BEHR-SIGEL, France
Dr. Kari Elisabeth BØRRESEN, Norway
Miss Julia CAMPOS, Mexico
Mrs. Catherine CHIOTELLIS, Greece
Dr. Sture CULLHED, Sweden
Mrs. Vasiliki ECKLEY, United States of America
Ms. Padmasini J. GALLUP, India
Dr. Catharina J. M. HALKES, Netherlands
Dr. Ursula KING, England
Miss Beatrice LUYOMBYA, Uganda
Mrs. Brigitte McLEOD, Federal Republic of Germany
Mrs. Carolina PATTIASINA, Indonesia
Dr. Yvonne PELLE-DOUEL, France
Dr. Maen PONGUDOM, Thailand
Dr. Bianca STORCHI-GORINI, Italy
Mr. Giampaolo GORINI, Italy
Pater Dr. Gerhard VOSS, Federal Republic of Germany

WCC STAFF

The Rev. Janet E. CRAWFORD, Assistant to the Community of Women and Men in the Church Study Desk
Miss Yvonne ITIN, Secretary, Community of Women and Men in the Church Study Desk
The Rev. Dr. Michael KINNAMON, Executive Secretary, Commission on Faith and Order
Dr. MASAMBA ma Mpolo, Executive Secretary, Office of Family Education
The Rev. Dr. Constance F. PARVEY, Director of the Community of Women and Men in the Church Study

Interpreters

Mrs. Tomoko EVDOKIMOFF
Mr. Robert FAERBER
Mrs. Roswitha GINGLAS-POULET
Mrs. Renate SBEGHEN

The Authority of Scripture

A woman...

that's the one who always has a bad conscience

because she is not somebody else

because she is not somewhere else

because she can't devote herself fully to her job, to politics, to her home, to her education, to her subjects, to her children, to society, to kindergartens, to school, to art, to culture, to the others, to the old people, to the sick people

because she can't relax completely

because she can't work wholeheartedly

because she is in bits and pieces, in many pieces

because she can't cope with women's fight for liberation

because she is still not the new woman, the solitary woman, the independent woman, the woman with her own life, her own identity.

A woman...

that's the one who has a bad conscience

because she has taken up too many tasks;

because she can't manage everything successfully;

because she is not doing anything wholeheartedly;

because she is running, jumping, driving, flying from here to there;

because she is occupied with trifles;

because she has a bad conscience for having a bad conscience.

But a woman... that's the one who really knows that her bad conscience is not bad at all; on the contrary

it is a sensitive, sensible, reasonable, right reaction to wrong conditions.

(Poem by Karin Lentz-translated from the Swedish)

INTRODUCTION

The consultation on "The Authority of Scripture in Light of the New Experiences of Women" was held in the Amsterdam Tropical Museum. The 25 official participants reflected the international setting, surrounded by art treasures and exhibitions from all over the world–from ancient boats of the South Pacific to video tapes of Calcutta's crowded streets. They came from 17 WCC member churches in 21 countries, almost equally balanced between North and South. Five participants were Roman Catholic. Missing from the dialogue, however, was the Orthodox contribution, an essential input for any future work on this theme.

Preliminary materials for the consultation set forth several goals or purposes:

- To explore the basic character of scriptural authority in different contexts and to consider its relationship to the new experiences of women.
- To describe the issues experientially rather than purely analytically, exposing the important relationship between scripture and culture.
- To examine the role that scripture has played, and continues to play, in supporting and vindicating male domination.
- To provide a forum for an exchange of experiences and perspectives in the form of a subject/subject dialogue rather than "objective" presentations.
- To prepare a working document to aid in clarifying the issues and to stimulate further dialogue in the churches on scriptural authority as part of the search for renewal of community in the church.

Most of the work in Amsterdam took place in small working groups. These groups drafted daily reports of their discussions, reports which have been edited by the Geneva staff in order to produce the following document. At some points, the actual language of the working group reports is used; at others, the reports are summarized and presented in the "third person". Between the sections of the final report are "dialogues", drawn directly from the working group material, which give some flavour of the actual "give and take" of the meeting.

In addition to the working groups, there were several short plenary presentations designed to enrich and focus the discussions.*

One final word of introduction: the Amsterdam consultation began as the world learned of the killings of the Maryknoll sisters in El Salvador. The participants requested that any publication of this report be made in their memory.

1. THE CONSULTATION

- "The Church thinks of authority in terms of limits and power. God has nothing to do with this sort of authority."
- "I view the Bible as that which can be rejected when it is not in accord with the demands of experience."
- "It was not 'authority' which I first discovered in scripture, but Jesus who exploded all authority."

These statements from the meeting raise questions of crucial importance for the church: To what extent, and on what basis, is the Bible authoritative for Christian reflection and action today? Can the Bible's authority, at times unquestioned, be reaffirmed in the face of legitimate challenges from contemporary experience, including the new experiences of women?

Such questions have played an important, if sometines overlooked, role in the ecumenical movement from its beginning. At the first Assembly of the World Council of Churches–Amsterdam 1948–women participants recommended that the teachings of scripture with reference to women be reconsidered as part of the necessary work of restoring the church to its wholeness. As a result of this initiative, studies were undertaken in the 1950s by the Commission on the Life and Work of Women in the Church, and later by the Department of Men-Women Relationships in Church and Society.

---

* These brief papers–by Catharina Halkes, Mariana Katoppo and Madeleine Boucher –are available upon request from the Faith and Order Secretariat in Geneva.

Meanwhile, the WCC (and especially the Faith and Order Commission) was carrying out a series of studies and conferences on scripture and scriptural authority as part of the search for visible church unity. Several of these reports have now been collected in *The Bible: Its Authority and Interpretation in the Ecumenical Movement* (Faith and Order Paper No. 99). At its 1978 meeting in Bangalore, the Faith and Order Commission acknowledged that the time had come to integrate these initiatives. Amsterdam 1980, the first WCC consultation dealing with scripture which takes the experiences of women as its starting point, is the result of this new awareness.

At Amsterdam 1980, women and men said:

> We, the delegates of this consultation, reaffirm the importance of these questions and express our appreciation for past efforts which have led to this new initiative by the Community Study of the Faith and Order Commission. We assert, however, that sufficient attention has not yet been given to the questions raised about biblical authority in light of the emerging self-understandings of women in church and society.
>
> Our experience at this consultation has been remarkably rich, in large part because our backgrounds are so varied. We are Protestants and Catholics, women and men, half from the northern and half from the southern hemisphere. Yet cutting across all the diversity has been the common affirmation that the Bible has been used to justify and maintain a view that women are, and should be, subordinate to men. Traditional, male-oriented interpretations of scripture have marginalized women, subordinating them to men in order of creation and stereotyping their roles and images in church and society, often relegating women, in the name of biblical authority, to a second class of humanity. Throughout the world a new awareness is growing, an awareness of the fundamental equality of persons and of the need for a new community of women and men that rejects patterns of hierarchical authority and power. These experiences must not be ignored by the church. Nor can they be ignored in discussions of biblical authority.
>
> At this consultation we began to discover–together, in community–a renewed vision of the authority of scripture. Biblical authority, seen in perspective of our experience, is not a buttress to the status quo, but a channel through which the witness to the

living God prophetically challenges us today. We have begun to discover the full importance of a multicultural discussion of this issue. Changes in the concept of biblical authority must respect the different cultural, social and ecclesiastical contexts in which we live.

Emerging from our five days of intense discussions were some simple, but important, affirmations:

- We stress the importance of viewing scripture as a whole and of attempting to discern its central themes–e.g. the acceptance and validation of all human beings. We affirm that the Bible's Good News of liberation and hope is far more important than the patriarchal world-view in which it is couched.
- We recognize, along with modern biblical scholarship, that there is always a cultural conditioning influencing us as we approach the Bible. The act of biblical interpretation thus inevitably involves the encounter of the text with the contexts.
- We acknowledge that, for those who accept the Christian faith, the Bible becomes an "authority", transforming our character and our view of reality. We welcome reflections on, and applications of, this authority because it grounds us in God's reign which is beyond all powers and principalities. We reject, however, an application of scriptural authority which tries to make Scripture a "rule book" for all questions of modern life.

The Amsterdam consultation could not have taken place without the initiative and help of a local working group which hosted the meeting and looked after all local arrangements, including a reception by the Amsterdam Council of Churches. They also raised the funds necessary to ensure that the meeting could be truly international.

The consultation expressed its appreciation in the following words:

> We who have participated in this consultation express our appreciation to the World Council of Churches and its Study on the Community of Women and Men in the Church for this opportunity to share our concerns across cultures. We also express our appreciation to the Amsterdam Working Group, composed of theological students and faculty at the Free University in Amsterdam, for its efforts which made this consultation possible. Without the financial resources made available through the efforts

of the Working Group, this meeting could not have had world-wide participation. The unique partnership between the Amsterdam Working group and the WCC Community Study serves as a model of local and international cooperation.

Dialogue 1: Shall we dance?

Many at the Amsterdam Consultation experienced tension between past authority and present experience. The old emphasis on words as conveyers of "truth" no longer seemed satisfactory because the authority of those words can no longer be taken for granted. This is an age when lived experience–movement, action, "dance"–has come to temper the authority of words. Most participants at this meeting acknowledged this shift in one way or another. But there was a question: How can we be creative and spontaneous, yet sensitive to those words from the past that speak authentically?

The following dialogue, recorded in one of the small working groups, reflects this tension and indicates how the people, mostly unknown to one another, tried to deal with it. The actual discussion took over twenty minutes. Neither the passion of the discussion nor the trust which emerged from it can be expressed in this retelling.

Moderator: "The nature of authority ... Well, this question is really three questions. Should we divide ourselves into three sub-groups, or stay together?"

Voice 1: "Oh, it would be sad to split ourselves. Aren't these questions really all part of the same issue? And doesn't that issue have to do with more than sub-groups and reports? I remember what was said earlier about how women should read poetry daily. We usually use only one way of expressing ourselves, and there are so many others. Why not use the first hour we have this afternoon to take off our shoes, move the table, and I can lead us in a circle dance–there's plenty of room. Then, after tea, we can talk about the question with refreshed minds."

(Lengthy pause)

Voice 2: "Please don't accuse me of simply being a North Atlantic male, but I'd like to remind us that we have a task ahead of us today that's very important. A report is the best way we can speak to others about these issues and I propose that we go at it by sharing our views."

Voice 3: "We have been 'going at' the Bible constantly. Can't we stop long enough to let it address us? To lose sight of our need to hear the texts themselves would be a distortion of our purpose here."

Voice 4: "I agree. I can no longer use words this afternoon. We ought to dance!"
Voice 5: "Suddenly I feel out of place. You may like to dance, but I do not. As far as I am concerned, I think it is wrong to impose something on others that is not their forte."
Voice 4: "But people are always imposing an intellectual methodology on those of us who don't want it! That's precisely the point."
Voice 5: "We were invited to a consultation. There is certainly a time and place for dance, but it's not now or here."
Voice 6: "I'm with you. We're here to talk about important issues. This whole thing has taken up a lot of time and energy."

(Lengthy pause)

Moderator: "Isn't there a compromise? Can't we use this dancing together as a kind of worship after our sessions?"
Voice 1: "That's repressive tolerance! Instead of really doing something different, we stick it off in a corner. I feel that I will be unable to participate in this group if we continue to work on a solely intellectual level."
Moderator: "That would be the worst thing of all! We must reach an agreement together, not threaten to split up."
Voice 2: "I agree, we must stay together. I still think we need to do a report, but I will do what the group decides. Maybe dancing would be a good thing for a while."
An agreement was reached that part of the group would dance until tea-time while the rest would simply carry on their conversation–in the same room. Most of the group danced, joining hands, forming a circle... And as they danced they sang–"Sarah's Circle"... Suddenty the door opened and a large, red-faced man entered.
Voice of authority: "Excuse me, but I've been trying to hold a meeting in the next room, and you are making quite a lot of noise. The walls here are very thin. I'm sure you understand."

2. WOMEN SPEAK: THE INTERACTION OF SCRIPTURE AND EXPERIENCE

A. Scripture: text and context

It became clear at Amsterdam, through the sharing of personal experiences in small working groups, that Scripture has frequently been used to reinforce the sexual stereotypes of a culture and that cultural patterns have been applied to reinforce patriarchal interpretations of scripture. As one African participant put it: "There is often an unholy alliance between a certain interpretation of biblical texts and the biases of a traditional culture. For example, in our situation, the Old Testament is frequently endorsed by traditional Africans who charge, on scriptural grounds, that the women's role is to breed children and that their place is in the kitchen. 'Here', he said, the principle of selective amnesia is at work, where people choose from scripture only what they like." This same problem was expressed by a voice from a Chinese culture:

> In the history of Christian mission to China, there is little acknowledgement of women missionaries. Recently there is some research on the history of women and ministry in China. It now becomes evident that the contributions by women missionaries and women in China have been denied and neglected.
>
> The relationships of men and women in the traditional Chinese family and society are quite similar to those of the ancient Jews of the New Testament times. Therefore, there is a similarity in the basic Chinese cultural pattern and the concept of women's subordination in the Pauline passages. These served as an excellent contact point for missionaries in the sharing of the biblical teaching because it makes the gospel sound less culturally offensive. This means that the constant use of these subordinating texts and traditional Chinese cultural patterns have been mutually reinforcing.
>
> In addition, with reference to language, the Chinese love to work from the concrete and the specific rather than the abstract. Such a preference affects their approach to biblical interpretation. For example, the Chinese prefer to look at specific images of women, such as the veil reference of St Paul in I Corinthians 11, and then to make generalizations and theology starting from specific images and situations. The negative consequence of this is that guiding principles that are more inclusive, such as Galatians 3:27-28 and Acts 2:17, are often overlooked.

In western culture, because it has been so shaped by Christianity, the specific interaction between text and context, church and society, is sometimes overlooked. The tension between the two, and the ways in which scripture is used to support negative cultural patterns, are more apparent in a culture that has not been so closely linked for centuries with Christian institutions and values. The following statement from an African participant about cultural roles and attitudes toward women and their interplay with scripture underscore this point:

> Our social context is difficult. Men are considered polygamous by nature, and because women do not want to see their husbands go to jail, many women are opposed to more severe legislation against adultery. Children are important according to the social values. The phrase "mother is supreme" is emphasized over against a childless woman, but once a wife, a woman almost becomes the property of her husband. She does not have the freedom to go out and do things that interest her. She has to work hard in her husband's home and fields; she must bear him children and feed them. This is her primary duty. If a man goes away, he often comes back and neglects his wife because they have grown apart. He does not want her anymore, and he may marry another woman... A single woman, or a woman without children, is unacceptable.
>
> In addition, a woman who does not give birth to a son is not only blamed, but has to suffer herself. With only daughters, a wife has not been able to live up to her husband's expectation and he can find this a justification for leaving her. A wife is not so important. There is always another one. Much more important to an African man is his mother. Finally, it can also be stated that, in terms of job and employment opportunities, there are several forms of discrimination against women: more difficulties to get a job, worse conditions, lower pay, no pension. Several biblical texts, both from the Creation story of the Old Testament and from the New Testament, particularly the epistles, are used to sanction these various situations.

Similarly, from the Caribbean, it was noted that, "Women and men work side by side in the fields or in their small industries from Monday to Saturday, but on Sunday they often go to church to be divided. It is said that for 'scriptural reasons' women sit on the left, men on the right."

These examples illustrate how cultural patterns that subjugate women have been justified by an appeal to distorted use of scripture which in turn has reinforced patterns of the cultural oppression of women. Christianity reflects an amalgam of many different traditions and cultures–first the Semitic, Judaic, Graeco-Roman traditions, later the North Atlantic, and much later the many Asian,

African and other diverse ethnic cultures and peoples of the world. An essential part of the ecumenical task today is to delineate what is intrinsically "Christian" through ages of intermingling Christian experience with various cultures, values and traditions.

The sharing at Amsterdam not only uncovered abuses, it also affirmed that slowly, often painfully, the images and roles of women are changing. The following observation and challenge came from a Latin American participant.

> Regarding women's image and participation, I can say from experience these two things are intimately related but they do not run parallel; or at least it is impossible to say one is before the other. Changing the image of what women are carries with it a change of attitude regarding what women do or can do, and at the same time (this is the more common experience) as women are observed in their new participation in church and society, their image changes. In this area, "church" and "society" are for me inseparable, complementary elements of a single reality. As women committed to our society from the viewpoint of our faith, we have a lot to say in what we do about our acceptance and our "image" in the church and in society.

B. Sexist use of scriptural authority

Is the Bible inherently sexist? This question provoked a lively discussion in Amsterdam. Some participants argued that it most certainly is, that the patriarchal setting in which the Bible was written has so permeated the text that its images of women, and attitudes towards women, are totally determined by a male perspective, a male projection of who women are. Others contended that, while certain passages do reveal the patriarchal bias of their authors and editors, the central themes of God's relevation in Scripture call for an inclusive community and a liberation of all humanity. All agreed, however, that the churches have often used scriptural texts to reinforce the subordination of women. Several participants shared personal examples of this subordination.

A woman from Latin America gave the following account:

> In my early experience I found that the exhortations and imperatives of I Corinthians 11 and 14, of Ephesians 5 and of I Timothy 2 were understood as rules for the church of today. Teaching from the life and ministry of Jesus was almost completely absent. An extreme example of this tendency is a church

group in which I spent four years of my youth, where the effort to "play first-century church" (as Krister Stendahl would put it) resulted in a rule of absolute silence for women in any meeting where men were present. Women were not allowed to pray aloud or even to read the scripture. We were taught on the basis of selected biblical texts that although men and women are equally *objects* of God's redemptive love, only men are fit *subjects* for expressing human response to God in worship and responsibility before God in teaching.

A man from Europe spoke of the struggle for the ordination of women, even in his "progressive" country. Despite the fact that there are approximately 400 ordained women (about 15% of the clergy) in the Church of Sweden, there remains a loud dissenting voice which bases its opposition on passages such as "women should remain quiet" (I Corinthians 14:34) and that certain "good works are proper for a woman" (I Timothy 2:11). Theological opposition to ordination, he noted, generally makes reference to the "proper order of creation" and "the order of salvation", quoting Genesis 2 and Ephesians 5 in particular. He emphasized that even men who support equal rights for women in secular fields often oppose women's ordination on the basis of an assumed biblical authority. There seems to be a kind of unspoken assumption that the secular status of women or men may change, but scripture is unchanging. An implication to be drawn from this is that sexism in society is not tolerated, but in the church it is justified on biblical grounds.

A woman from Asia described how her questionnaire, designed to gain information in preparation for this consultation, led to actual combat in an Indian Christian village–the women arguing that Jesus spoke to them of liberation, the men claiming a scriptural warrant to beat the women and silence them in public. Christianity may have made the traditionally low estate of women in Indian society even worse, she argued, because claims of male domination are now "supported" by sacred text. The authority of Hinduism rests on its "way of life", she explained, but Christianity can too easily give authority to cultural oppression by using scripture with a sexist bias.

Because of different contexts, not all participants saw discrimination against women in quite the same way. A voice from the Middle East points out that "in Arabic, the terminology concerning men and women is less sharply differentiated, less 'aggressive' than in the

West. In society, there is a deep respect for the woman. Notwithstanding certain forms of discrimination, the authority of women is real in many fields."

One voice regarded the issue of subjugation and sexual stereotyping in Scripture as far less important than other social and economic problems.

> One almost always reads the Bible with a biased viewpoint. ... My problem as an African woman is not to seek biblical texts justifying the position of women in one sense or another. The African woman has a problem she has to resolve–that is finding something with which to nourish her children. This is her first preoccupation. Once this problem is resolved, the conscientization of woman to her condition will be automatic. To look for biblical texts on the subject of women can be interesting, but for the moment it is, as I see it, not productive.

From still another part of the world, a voice from Eastern Europe brought a reminder that society is often far ahead of the church when it comes to encouraging equality in women/men relationships.

> There was a great change in our life after World War II. Women had to learn to live rather independently. Young Christian people had to encounter a new school system with the challenge to confessing their Christian faith. In our socialist society, equal rights for women and men are guaranteed. In societal life, men and women have grown accustomed to working together in "mixed groups". Only in this way is it possible really to advance. This means that the polarization between the sexes is less emphasized. ... A fundamentalist interpretation of the Bible is considered a main obstacle to developing new forms of relationship.

These testimonies, among others shared by participants in Amsterdam, bear witness to the need for a continued discussion of scriptural authority and its use in church and society. It is not easy to achieve new levels of understanding today, as the lengthy discussions at Amsterdam point out. We (like all "interpreters") bring the full weight of our experience and culture to the biblical text. For many of us this means bringing our experience as women into a world mostly dominated by men. For all of us, women and men, it means contributing our experience to the search for renewed human community, keeping always before us the fact that priorities are not the same worldwide.

C. Scripture as a basis for renewed community

1. Women and the Hebrew scriptures

It was frequently said in Amsterdam that certain passages of the Hebrew scriptures (Old Testament) are used to keep women in an inferior position, passages that do not warrant such interpretation. Among those most often abused are:

- The story of Eve as created second–a "helper" under the rule of her husband–and the temptation story (Genesis 2 and 3) are sometimes used as an argument for women's subordination to man in creation and man's role as an authority over woman.
- The purification laws of Leviticus relating to the uncleanness of menstruating and child-bearing women have been used to keep women out of central ritual functions. Even today, in some societies, menstruating women are considered "unclean" and, hence, are not allowed to go to church, to handle "holy things", or to receive the Holy Communion. Rites of purification for women are also still practised in some churches and areas of the world, signifying that women are by nature "unclean"; but no parallel Levitical laws are invoked for men.
- Woman as the image of unfaithfulness is sometimes seen as a major Old Testament archetype. Israel itself is imaged as a harlot, or wayward wife (Ezekiel 22 and Hosea 2). It is the woman who is portrayed as unfaithful, not the man.

In contrast to these texts from Hebrew Scriptures, used to stress woman's inferiority, there are also passages that present women as indispensable leaders–strong, willing to confront injustice and to challenge entrenched authority. Three obvious examples are Miriam "the prophet" (Exodus 15), Deborah the judge and general of early Israel (Judges 4 and 5), and Huldah, the authoritative interpreter of the Deuteronomic Law (II Kings 22 and II Chronicles 34).

Just as important, yet often overlooked, are the female images for divine authority. The imagery of God as a loving Mother (Hosea 11, Isaiah 49. Deuteronomy 32:8) needs to be emphasized, but without falling into a distorted imagery which puts "Mother" on a pedestal while requiring her to be submissive (a parallel to some interpretations of Mary, the Virgin and Enthroned Mother). In addition, a desire was expressed in Amsterdam to go beyond the role concepts of God as "Father" or "Mother" and to speak of God with qualities such as "mild, warm, loving"–the way in which God is revealed in

Exodus 34:6 (the manifestation to Moses), or in Ezekiel 34 (the Good Shepherd).

The consultation discovered that, in moving beyond the patriarchy in Hebrew scriptures, the texts can offer more help in the search for inclusive community than has been generally recognized. One of the working groups asked, "Where did Jesus, as fully human, find his vision of love and equality?" The answer was: "From Amos, Malachi, Isaiah and the other great prophets of ancient Israel." It was urged that more work be done in this area of biblical research to rediscover the positive texts which have been overlooked and forgotten.

2. Women and the New Testament

Many felt that the New Testament witness has shaped our understanding of women and men in new community in some positive ways. The following examples were cited:

- Jesus' injunction, in Matthew 23, to "call no one Father" offers a model of human authority that is neither aggressive nor competitive, neither distant nor hierarchial.
- Jesus' most significant theological truths were made known to women; e.g. Jesus revealed his Messiahship to a woman (John 4) and women were the first to witness to the resurrection.
- Jesus made an effort–as with Mary and Martha (Luke 10) and the Samaritan women (John 4)–to seek out women and to accept their full collaboration. He also defended women and refused to condemn them (John 8 and Luke 7), and he did not set the woman "with the issue of blood" apart, but he healed her (Luke 8, Mark 5, Matthew 9).
- Romans 16:1 refers to Phoebe as a "minister" of the church, using the same word Paul uses to describe himself as a "minister". They were equally "diakonos".

Many participants noted that for them the Gospels witness more to a relationship of liberation between women and men than the Epistles, though there are exceptions (e.g. Galatians 3:27-28) which provide fundamental principles for this new relationship. Some passages in the Epistles were frequently mentioned as having a negative impact on women, particularly I Corinthians 11 and 14, Ephesians 5 and I Timothy 2.

There were also some reflections on approaches to the texts related to Mary. It was expressed that the person of Mary is often interpreted from two texts: Luke 1:38 (divine fiat) and Luke 2:51 (pondering everything in her heart). Some suggested that care should be taken to consider Mary's life as a whole. Others felt that select texts about Mary, such as those about the mother of Jesus (e.g. John 2 and 18), should be seen in the larger context of Mary's symbolic aetiological role in church and tradition.

Certain biblical texts were found helpful for envisioning new community. They are not presented here as "proof texts", but as suggestions for theological reflection which may enable the liberating power of scripture to break through our human relationships as women and men:

Genesis 1:27-28(women and men created equal)
Exodus 15:20-21(Miriam)
Exodus 34:6 (God as gracious and loving)
Deuteronomy 32:8, Hosea 11, Isaiah 66:13 (God as feminine)
Judges 4-5 (Deborah)
Matthew 15:21-28, Mark 7:24-30 (the Cananite woman)
Matthew 23:8-12 (call no one Father)
Luke 1:46-56 (the Magnificat)
Luke 7:36-50 (Jesus anointed by the sinful woman)
Luke 10:38-42 (Mary and Martha)
Luke 15:8-10 (the lost coin–woman as example)
John 4:1-44 (the Samaritan woman)
John 8:1-11 (the woman caught in adultery)
John 20:1-10, Mark 16:1-8 (women as witnesses at the tomb)
Acts 18:2 (Priscilla)
Romans 16:1-7 (Phoebe)
I Corinthians 12:12-31 (the one body)
Galatians 3:27-28 (neither male nor female)
I Peter 2:4-5 (the holy priesthood)

An obvious question raised by this experiential exploration of scripture was: Can we accept some passages and reject others? Does this not undermine the authority of the Bible as a whole? In addition, contextual priorities worldwide are not the same. In a divided church and a divided world, on what basis is scripture unifying and universal? This led us to our discussion on the authority of the Bible.

Dialogue 2: By what authority?

What is the nature of scriptural authority? What is its relation to other "authorities" in our lives? The following voices, drawn from all three of the working groups, indicate how some women and men at Amsterdam viewed these questions.

Voice 1: "The church thinks of authority in terms of limits and power. God has nothing to do with this sort of authority. The question is: How do our experiences affect our views of biblical authority?"

Voice 2: "My educational experience growing up in the Caribbean led me to a sense of equality with men which was belied in the church where only men are accorded positions of authority. This led me back to the scripture where I discovered liberation, particularly in the example of Jesus."

Voice 3: "I learned from feminist theology that we must invest things around us with whatever authority they possess and that our experience as women does not need the legitimation of scripture. I view the Bible as a partner in dialogue which can be rejected when it is not in accord with my experience. In our western European context, I have not found the scripture necessarily liberating, in fact it has often been used to oppress."

Voice 4: "Because of my own struggles with the debilitating male imagery of western culture, our issue speaks to me personally. I have sought answers in such places as psychoanalysis, but found that the liberating side of scripture was much more of a help and spoke to me more 'authoritatively', because it is rooted in the universal framework of God's activity."

Voice 5: "For me, authority itself is a problem. I was raised in a context where the authority of God seemed linked with the authority of my father, and where Christian authority in general seemed to set limits on who I could be."

Voice 6: "Scriptural authority is tied to our estimate of Christ. For me, Christ is the love which triumphs over evil, the model of authority in servanthood and, as such, Christ is the essence of the scriptural witness. Speaking as a man and a theologian, I can see that the new situation of women in the secular world demands that the traditional understanding of women in scripture be challenged."

For some, authority itself was oppressive; for others, the search for authority in their lives became a way of liberation. For all, authority is linked with power–oppressive, patriarchial power, or liberating power in Christ.

3. BIBLICAL AUTHORITY RECONSIDERED

Allowing community to be built was central to the planning of the Amsterdam consultation. Questions about biblical authority were posed within the groups, which themselves struggled to realize new forms of organization and "authority". This procedure necessarily led to a variety of approaches, six of which are outlined below. These approaches are not abstract and unrelated categories, but overlapping emphases that grow out of shared experiences. They bear witness to the fact that no single method can be all-encompassing. Despite the variety of starting points, there was a united conviction that as biblical authority is reconsidered, the new experiences of women must be central to this reconsideration.

A. Towards a renewed definition of authority

A major priority of this consultation was to re-evaluate the concept of authority itself. The term provoked a wide range of heated reactions: some identified the word with stability and continuity, but many regarded "authority" with suspicion, linking it with images of militarism and governmental oppression, or with forms of hierarchy, status quo and inflexibility in the church. The different cultural, political and confessional backgrounds of participants made neat definitions of the term impossible. Connotations ranged from those of personal authority to authoritarianism to benevolent authority.

Given this range, the consultation nevertheless agreed that true authority–biblically-based authority–is not to be understood as dominating, subjugating power. The model for true authority must find its centre in the life and teachings of Jesus and his exercise of authority as service and love. Such passages as Matthew 23:11-12 were mentioned: "The greatest among you must be your servant. For whoever exalts himself will be humbled; and whoever humbles himself will be exalted" (see also Luke 22:24-27). It was pointed out that the character of authority is that of a summons: the Divine addressing the human situation that God's message of love (John 13:34-35) and justice (Matthew 6:33-34) might be fulfilled.

Further, it was stressed that authority, as perceived in the Bible, and as exemplified by Jesus, must have a particular "human face". Real authority eschews the legalism which Jesus and Paul so adamantly opposed. Real authority rests on one's sensitivity to particular human needs. It is a sensitivity patterned on the exercise of authority by Jesus, the Christ – e.g. in the forgiving of sins (Mark 2:10) and healing (Luke 11:14-20).

It is true that Jesus appealed to the authority of scripture, but he also challenged the use of scriptural authority when necessary, as in the story when the devil tempts him by quoting scripture (Matthew 4:5-10). This was also the case in his teaching: "You have heard what was said to the men of old, but I say ..." (Matthew 5:22ff). It was the living authority of Jesus that the people recognized and could accept. His words liberated people from "words" and "laws". He reversed the rules of the so-called religious order, saying that the Sabbath was made for the people, and not the people for the Sabbath.

This understanding of authority, found so clearly in the text itself, must surely be applied to the way the text is taught and used today. To speak of the authority of scripture as if its precepts could be imposed legalistically without constant dialogue between the text and contemporary experience, is to belie the basis, the Living Christ, upon which that authority is claimed.

The link between biblical authority and other authorities in our lives is so strong that a fresh understanding of the former must take account of our new relationships in family, church and society (see Matthew 5:17-48). Experience teaches us that true authority can never be imposed; it only works when it is offered, chosen and freely accepted. Genuine religious authority must not be confused with fidelity to hierarchicalism or legalism. Rather, it arises out of sharing and dialogue. Such authority is difficult to describe; but we can say that it involves a relationship between the person (or the text) in "authority" and the person who chooses to receive it. It involves, as one group put it, a "listening into speech" through which people are enabled to find ways of feeling, speaking, and understanding their own identity in relation to the other. It involves a dialectic, a "vibrating between persons", such as that found in the interaction of "leader" and "partner" in a dance.

Within the church, this means that authority is grounded not in ecclesiastical hierarchy, but has its source in the believing community itself. Within the church as the body of Christ, everyone is contributing – women and men, lay and ordained. The eye cannot say to the hand "I have no need of you" since each member is indispensable to the authority of the whole. Real authority emerges from the co-ordinated gifts of all the members. Each is accorded full dignity.

Within this community, scripture has an authoritative role; but this role must be understood in the light of the Bible's original oral tradition, the telling and retelling of the story. The Word became flesh. This witness is conveyed through specific stories, dialogues, remembrances of people's actions. The early Christian community was involved in the shaping of the text itself, "living the scripture" by telling and living its story in many different, changing circumstances. Today the Bible remains as a book of witness among us, a source of continual dialogue. Its genuine authority is shaped and re-shaped in the community.

It is possible, of course, that even though new meanings are given to old words (e.g. "authority"), the previous negative connotations continue to recur as long as the word is used. The participants recommended, therefore, that other terms also be sought. Some attention might be given to such phrases as "dialogue with scripture" or "inspired by scripture" or "a relationship of faithfulness with scripture". These have the advantage of implying a dynamic encounter between the reader, the text, and the One God whose Spirit informs both.

B. Towards a clarification of the basis for biblical authority

A second approach builds on the previous attempts of the Faith and Order Commission to articulate and clarify the possible bases of biblical authority. The working groups at Amsterdam suggested that there are at least six possible entry points for viewing the authority of scripture.

1. The Bible is authoritative because it is the inspired Word of God. Within this category fall a wide range of doctrines. Inspiration may be understood, for example, as direct "dictation" or as the operation of the Holy Spirit through fallible, human authors. It must be noted that, even if scripture serves as the medium of God's Word, it need not be directly identified with it.

2. The Bible is a witness of God's liberating power, the authority of which does not belong to the text *per se,* but comes through the power of its witnesses to lead people to faith.

3. The Bible is authoritative in that, as the determinative record of the early church, it is the document by which the church defines itself and it is a primary source of the church's worship and teaching.

4. The Bible is the primary source of human ethical wisdom, a source for the behavioural norms of people, communities, and

societies, and, as such, can be appealed to as an important moral/ ethical authority.

5. The Bible is authoritative in that it is the most, or one of the most, influential literacy documents, a rich compendium of ancient texts providing stories, myths, metaphors, poetry and paradigms that help interpret human experience through its history, teachings, worship, doctrinal and spiritual development.

6. The Bible has no special claim to authority.

Many at the Amsterdam consultation found the second option (2) appealing because it allows us to speak of the Bible's unique, revelatory authority while still leaving room for the vital witness of contemporary experience in widely divergent contexts. In the report of the 1971 Faith and Order Commission meeting in Louvain, this option received significant attention. According to this study, the Bible may be seen as authoritative because "by its witness it makes possible the knowledge of God and of [God's] authority. Therefore it only has derived authority. Nevertheless, anyone who has once encountered the living God in Christ in the Bible will again and again return to this source." Interpretations of scripture which have led to abuses against women, as mentioned earlier, actually undermine the authority of scripture because they prevent the Bible from fully revealing God's liberating Word and, thus, from leading women and men forward in faith. To ignore the experience of those who have been subjugated and oppressed in the name of scripture is to undermine the genuine claims of biblical authority. The temptation of Jesus serves as a reminder of this. The devil himself quotes scripture in attempting to undermine Jesus' identity and vocation.

C. Towards an identification of the "essence of scripture"

The first two entry points imply a third. Some participants sought to identify fundamental thrusts, themes, directions in scripture by which the witness of its various parts could be evaluated. Most agreed that one central witness of scripture is God's identification with the poor, the outcast, the oppressed–among which are women as a "sub-caste" according to sex. Throughout scripture, God is revealed as a liberating force that calls both the powerful and the powerless to freedom and responsibility. There is strong support for this view today within the global church. The church in faithfulness to the Gospel must be in solidarity with the poor; we have a biblical mandate to search for a "just, participatory and sustainable society".

While this theme may not provide fully objective criteria for distinguishing among biblical texts and their seeming contradictions, they are more than subjective observations. It is not far-fetched to argue that Galatians 3:27-28 is closer to the central intentions of scripture than I Timothy 2:11-12, for scripture gives witness, through Christ, to the God who gives freedom. Therefore, scripture is affirmed and its authority is reinforced when its authority is used to promote the dignity and freedom of all human beings, which means the full inclusion of those who have been marginalized. The quoting of individual texts for the purpose of subordinating some groups (e.g. slaves, women, marginalized peoples) within church or society is an application of "words" of authority rather than an expression of the "spirit" of authority revealed in scripture and manifest in Christ.

The Amsterdam consultation affirmed that the Bible speaks to us in a fresh, authentic way, proclaiming a liberating word for both sexes. That word is not necessarily found in individual texts (though there are many which are positive toward women, as indicated earlier) but in the fundamental revelation of God's liberating Word that challenges all forms of inhumanity. Revelation is here experienced as a revolutionary impulse which empowers people to rebel against oppression and–through their encounter with the One God who creates, redeems and delivers–to become new community.

D. Towards a renewed understanding of interpretation

Still another entry point rests on the realization that the question of biblical authority is inextricably linked with hermeneutics, one's methods of interpretation. The working groups found that two axioms of modern biblical scholarship help us to clarify the steps towards an authentic vision of scriptural authority.

1. The biblical text must be understood in its historical context. God's Word is "incarnational", embedded in a specific place and time. This insight is the corner-stone of modern biblical criticism, yet its implications for the authority of Scripture–particularly in relation to women–must be repeated again and again. It is important to realize that Galatians 3:27-28 is not simply an eschatological promise of the future, but an ecclesiological reality of our baptism, a baptismal affirmation of the primitive church that stresses our present equality as members of Christ's body. A full understanding of Paul's admonitions in I Corinthians 11 and 14 that women keep

veiled and silent in the church must acknowledge the apostle's specific short-term aim to curb the confusion in the Corinthian congregation; they were probably not intended as biblical principles or norms regarding "women's place" in the church.

Full account must be taken of the fact that the Bible was written in the midst of a patriarchal society by men who were conditioned by their culture and social structures to view women as subordinate. It is remarkable that, given this context, the message of liberation is heard at all. For the sake of the Bible's authority, its patriarchal contexts cannot be allowed to obscure God's revelation that through baptism into a new community we are freed from bondage and called to live with Christ as Christ lived, in justice and love.

2. Interpretation occurs in the encounter of the biblical text, embedded as it is in its historical context, with readers who are also embedded in a particular historical moment. A fully "objective" interpretation of scripture is therefore impossible because no interpreter, or community of interpreters, can be divorced from the prejudices that accompany his/her immersion in time. Interpretation, then, involves a constant dialogue between the experience of the text and the experience of those who interpret. This understanding does not rule out the operation of the Holy Spirit in understanding scripture; rather, it locates this operation precisely in the ever new encounter of contemporary context and historical text.

It is clear that the authority of the Bible cannot be based on some hypothetical "objective reading"; rather, it grows out of living encounters with scripture. Our experience constitutes a vital partner in the unending dialogue with God's living Word. The consultation affirmed the importance of modern scholarship which stresses that the Bible was not written in a vacuum, but is formed by a particular historical time, and in a particular cultural and linguistic context. In this way, the Bible is an expression of God's incarnational approach to creation: the Word made flesh. We discover the meaning and authority of scripture as it lives among us, challenges us, and takes shape incarnationally through and with our experience.

The Amsterdam consultation affirmed, in short, that the Bible must be seen as a whole. It is a collection of testimonies in varied forms–narratives, histories, poems, proverbs, letters–which together provide a common witness of the people of God. It is a witness to the saving acts of God as experienced by the Hebrew and early Christian communities. It is a witness to their experience of themselves with

God and to the meaning this revelation gave to their community life. The Bible can never be separated from either the believing community from which it arose or the present believing community which encounters it. We read the Bible, therefore, not as a book of rules, but as a living testimony of God's concrete authority in history with which we must wrestle.

E. Towards an understanding of the need for biblical authority

Finally, many participants sought to articulate, in a more general way, both the need for and the limits of biblical authority. It was acknowledged that it is not only difficult, but probably dangerous, to avoid struggling with different views and experiences of authority. The participants searched for an understanding of authority to which they could appeal in common, one that was beyond all human institutions. The question became not how to avoid authority altogether, but how to discover an authentic authority that is justice and mercy for all peoples.

The decision to believe in Jesus Christ is a conscious choice, made in faith. Once we respond in faith to the witness of scripture, once we enter into the life of the Christian community, then scripture does become an authority for our lives. This is not to argue that the Bible becomes a norm for answering every question; but the Bible is an entry point to the primary witness to God's revelation in Jesus Christ, and, as such, it can shape our very approach to reality. The Bible is authority, as the early church said, that is sufficient unto faith. Yet scripture as authority is not static, but dynamic. The scriptural witness comes alive as it is in constant dialogue with contemporary experience.

It is through particular experience that God's ongoing presence is revealed in our lives. This means not only that contemporary experience helps interpret scripture but that such experience may be reflected upon from the perspective of the prophetic voice of scripture. For 2000 years scripture has frequently been improperly used to support oppression (including the oppression and subordination of women), but it has also served to call people to a new liberty beyond political and economic structures, to God's universal message of deliverance and new creation. Within scripture itself is much criticism of authority and its use and abuse, including scriptural authority. It calls into being the authentic authority of the living

Word, the fulfilling of the Messianic hope within and through our human, historical, temporal existence.

The authority of scripture is discovered and affirmed as the Bible is read, studied, explained, taught, proclaimed and lived in Christian community. Just as it is empty to speak of biblical interpretation apart from the encounter with contemporary experience, so the affirmation of scriptural authority is empty unless it serves to transform concrete relationships in the midst of community.

Such transformation is the final test of authority. If the surrounding society sees renewal in Christian communities - sees a liberating presence and power in their corporate existence - then it may accept that authentic authority is at work in their midst.

This authority was at work in communities of believers of the early church. The participants at the Amsterdam consultation affirmed their relationship to these writings and to the God they celebrate, saying:

> As we bring our corporate existence to our reading, we encounter the corporate experience of these ancient brothers and sisters. Like them, we attempt to respond to God's call–sometimes with courage and strength, sometimes with weakness and fear, always in relation to our neighbour.
>
> Authority, we observe, has to do with the Latin "augere"–to expand, to grow, to make space, to increase. When applied from above, vertically, it is oppressive, but when it happens horizontally it expands, "bursts"–not in an exclusive way, but inclusively. This kind of authority cannot be reduced to formulas that are given once and for all. Rather, it must continually be discovered and affirmed in creative struggle. We relate the biblical test to our experience and out of this encounter come new experiences, actions, and reflection. The dynamics of this biblical authority are difficult to describe, but we affirm that such a creative encounter with God's living Word is possible under the guidance of the Holy Spirit.
>
> Therefore, in obedience to the liberating message of scripture, we plead for a liberation of scripture that can transform our lives and our communities.

F. Towards authority in community

Because of the problem surrounding the word "authority", there is a need for discussion of authority with a view to arriving at a genuinely biblical understanding of it, dissociating authority from oppressive power.

The concept of authority is not easy to define. It takes diverse forms–sometimes insidious, as in the powerful and influential world of advertising–at other times crude and physically ruthless, as when it is linked with oppressive military regimes. A neat definition of authority can itself be "authoritarian" in that it may not fit every situation.

The understanding of authority will vary in different cultural settings. In one culture, country or group, authority may be accepted without difficulty, while in others it may have a questionable history. In Europe, for example, there is a long history–going back to Roman and feudal times–of the word being linked with patriarchal power, and exercised by men in power to oppress others. In Africa, tribal culture, corporate in character, located authority in the clan, with concepts of distributive justice as part of the clan system. In many Latin American countries and in southern Africa, authority is linked with militarism and economic/cultural oppression. In some countries, churches are also linked with the oppressive authority of the state and may wield power on the side of the state against the majority of the population, including their own church members.

All of this indicates that we are compelled to place the question of biblical authority in a very wide context. The issue is not simply that of a contrast between patriarchal and matriarchal systems, but of the continual quest for righteousness and love. The story of Sarah and Abraham was lifted up as one where both patriarchal and matriarchal systems are called into question because of the double oppression of Hagar who is both a woman and a slave, and neither the "patriarchal" Abraham nor the "matriarchal" Sarah questioned their right to use her. The story is all the more tragic in that it is still repeated, in new forms, in our own era when wives do not produce heirs. In some cultures, husbands can divorce for this reason, or take a second wife. In the search for renewed community, the consultation identified with the countless Hagars around the globe and examined itself for modes of servanthood that are mutual and just.

A new vision of authority of sripture in community must take seriously the "whole peoples of God" where there is "neither Jew nor Greek, there is neither slave nor free, there is neither male nor female, for all are one in Christ Jesus". This image of the people of God is inclusive. It is not confined to the exclusive limits of sex, class, race, but is, in its highest form, a reflection of the incarnate love of God in full, reconciled community.

In the search for renewed community, it was realized that our goals, structures and actions must be based on affirmations such as the following:

- Both women and men are equally objects of God's love and subjects for expressing God's witness.
- The people of God reflect a variety of gifts; there must be no sexual stereotyping or subordination of one person or group to another.
- In all thought and action, the people of God must take into account the complexities of human issues – including sex, race, class and cultural distinctions – as well as the economic, political and social structures in which women and men live.
- The people of God must acknowledge and celebrate the meaning brought to scripture through daily experiences.
- There is thus a necessary interchange between God's Word and the actual conditions of human life as a process through which the Holy Spirit can lead us to a deeper understanding of the authority of scripture in daily life. The participants stated: "Our vision is hopeful, but we are aware of the obstacles we encounter in realizing it."

DANCE GIVES HOPE

The opening plenary was a presentation in dance (also using music and slides) of Luke 7:36–50 by Rose Marie Tillisch of Denmark. Her portrayal was of the woman who anointed the feet of Jesus while he was dining with Simon and other Pharisees.

The setting for this presentation was not a village in first century Galilee, but modern Denmark. Jesus greets his host, sitting at table in the green garden of a Danish suburban home. The woman who comes to anoint his feet with oil is portrayed as a prostitute. Rose Marie, in dance, interprets her life – her loneliness, her struggle, her games of being "playgirl", her emptiness and longing.

The following excerpts from the discussion provoked by Rose Marie's presentation give a glimpse of how both the text and its "new" context were received:

"That she is a sinner is a caricature of a woman: how do we know that this woman was a prostitute?"

"From an exegetical point of view, this drama is not "orthodox", but all the same, this woman is the happiest because she has given a lot."

"Why is it that in preaching on these stories they do not speak to us–do not come through to us? Where is the short circuit? How do we move from exegesis to story?"

"Being forbidden to speak is a women's issue."

"A prostitute is a woman in an extreme situation. We do not identify with her. How can we become a person so identified with the oppressed?"

"Jesus let himself be touched by this unclean woman; it was not to his advantage."

"She is an assertive woman. She was serving a function in a patriarchal society. Men often don't even see their sin. These men with Jesus don't think they are sinning."

"There is an inner poverty in this story, material and spiritual."

"She is wearing the colour white. White does not give hope. But when she dances, dance gives hope."

LIST OF PARTICIPANTS

Dr. Rachel ANGOGO, Lutheran, Kenya
Sister Adeline ASFOUR, Roman Catholic, Lebanon
Ms. Mabel G. de BARIDON, Waldensian, Uruguay
The Rev. Hyacinth BOOTHE, Methodist, Jamaica
Professor Madeleine BOUCHER, Roman Catholic, USA
Ms. Agatha CHAN, Methodist, Hong Kong
Mrs. Jyotsna CHATTERJI, Church of South India, India (Moderator)
The Rev. Aldo COMBA, Waldensian, Switzerland
Professor Irene Westling FOULKES, Costa Rica
Professor Richard FOULKES, Costa Rica
Dr. Lucas GROLLENBERG, Roman Catholic, Netherlands
Dr. Catharina J. M. HALKES, Roman Catholic, Netherlands
Mrs. Agnès KABONGO, Church of Christ, Zaîre
Ms. Marianne KATOPPO, Presbyterian, Indonesia
Mr. Alberto Moisés MENDEZ, Baptist, Mexico
The Rev. Dr. Kjell Ove NILSSON, Church of Sweden, Sweden
Professor J. S. POBEE, Anglican, Ghana
Ms. Maria Teresa PORCILE-SANTISO, Roman Catholic, Uruguay
The Rev. Ursula RADKE, Federation of Protestant Churches, German Democratic Republic

The Rev. Nelida (Nelly) RITCHIE, Methodist, Argentina
The Rev. Gianna SCICLONE, Waldensian, Italy
Dr. Anne M. SQUIRE, United Church of Canada, Canada
The Rev. Rose Marie TILLISCH, Church of Denmark, Denmark
Ms. Fokkelien VAN DIJK, Netherlands
Ms. Rachel Conrad WAHLBERG, Lutheran Church in America, USA

Interpreters:	Mrs. Tomoko EVDOKIMOFF Mrs. Christine MÉAR
Amsterdam Working Group:	Dr. Sijbolt NOORDA Ms. Martine BAKEMA Ms. Ineke BAKKER Mr. Henk HORTENSIUS Ms. Gé SPEELMAN
Consultant:	Mrs. Nadine HUNDERTMARK, World YWCA, Switzerland
Observers:	Dr. Mario de BARIDON, Waldensian, Uruguay The Rev. Katherine KINNAMON, Disciples, USA
Press:	Ms. Kathy LOWE, England
CWMC Staff:	Ms. Jodi AUVIN The Rev. Janet E. CRAWFORD Miss Yvonne ITIN The Rev. Dr. Michael KINNAMON The Rev. Dr. Constance F. PARVEY

SELECT BIBLIOGRAPHY

The study book

Study on the Community of Women and Men in the Church, Geneva, WCC, 1978. Also available in French, German and Spanish. North American edition: New York, Friendship Press, 1978.

Group reports

Moss, Rachel (ed.), *God's Yes to Sexuality: Towards a Christian Understanding of Sex, Sexism and Sexuality*. The report of a working group appointed by the British Council of Churches. London, Fount Paperbacks, 1981.
Women in a Changing World, N°. 10, June 1981. Newsletter. Excerpts from local group reports. Available from Women in Church and Society, WCC.

Regional reports

Reports from consultations held in Africa, Asia, Europe, Latin America, Middle East and North America are available upon request from the Faith and Order Commission, WCC.

Specialized consultations

Parvey, Constance (ed.), *Ordination of Women in Ecumenical Perspective* (Faith and Order Paper N° 105), Geneva, WCC, 1980.

Sheffield consultation

Parvey, Constance F. (ed.), *The Community of Women and Men in the Church: A Report of the World Council of Churches' Conference, Sheffield, England, 1981,* Geneva, WCC, 1983. The official report.
Thompson, Betty, *A Chance to Change: Women and Men in the Church,* Geneva, WCC, 1983/Philadelphia, Fortress Press, 1982. A popular account.